Effective
Learning Objectives, Task-Setting and Differentiation

Professor Trevor Kerry

Note on Series Editor

Professor Trevor Kerry is well known for his books on the practice of teaching. He was formerly a senior LEA Adviser in charge of in-service training, and more recently has been a consultant and lecturer on aspects of education management. He holds a Visiting Fellowship in the University of East Anglia, and is a Vice-President of the College of Teachers. He sustains his contact with the classroom by teaching on a regular basis and is an Ofsted trained inspector.

Orders: please contact Bookpoint Ltd, 39 Milton Park, Abingdon, Oxon OX14 4TD. Telephone: (44) 01235 400414, Fax: (44) 01235 400454. Lines are open from 9.00 – 6.00, Monday to Saturday, with a 24 hour message answering service. Email address: orders@bookpoint.co.uk

British Library Cataloguing in Publication Data
A catalogue record for this title is available from The British Library.

ISBN 0 340 74790 0

First published 1999
Impression number   10 9 8 7 6 5 4 3 2 1
Year   2004 2003 2002 2001 2000 1999

Typeset by Transet Limited, Coventry, England.
Printed in Great Britain for Hodder & Stoughton Educational, a division of Hodder Headline Plc, 338 Euston Road, London NW1 3BH by Cox & Wyman, Reading, Berkshire

Contents

List of activities

List of tables

List of Figures

Statement of principles

The books in this series are based on a particular philosophy of teaching, which was largely developed (but not fossilised) in the 1980s as a result of the Teacher Education Project in the Universities of Nottingham, Leicester and Exeter – of which the series editor was Co-ordinator. This philosophy has stood the test of time and, it is argued, better meets the needs of teachers as professionals than some more recent developments, such as some competence models, which tend to trivialise the art and science of teaching. The principles of this philosophy are as stated:

Practical teaching consists of skills

- Skills can be isolated and identified
- Skills can be broken down into component parts
- Skills can be studied and taught
- Skills can be learned
- Skills can be reflected upon and refined
- Skills can be evaluated and assessed.

Each book takes a particular teaching skill and uses the latest research and practice to illuminate it in ways of immediate interest to all teachers.

Editorial: Skills for the future

The pace of change in society is constantly accelerating. This change is reflected in the world of education. Indeed, Drucker sums it up like this:

> *Every few hundred years in Western history there occurs a sharp transformation ... Within a few short decades, society re-arranges itself – its worldview; its basic values; its social and political structures; its arts, its key institutions. Fifty years later, there is a new world ... We are currently living through such a transformation.*
>
> **(Drucker, P (1993) Post-Capitalist Society. New York: Harper Business, p1)**

> *What will be taught and learned; how it will be taught and learned; who will make use of schooling; and the position of the school in society – all of this will change greatly during ensuing decades. Indeed, no other institution faces changes as radical as those that will transform the school.*
>
> **(Drucker, op. cit. p209)**

Yet it could be argued that even these changes have been modest in scope and pace compared with the changes that are likely to occur in the early years of the twenty-first century. Already the portents are visible of events which may affect radically *Schools for the Future*. These are just some of the changes of the recent past:

- the advent of the new learning technologies
- consumer choice and its implications for schools
- a re-definition of the nature of schools in the education process
- the changing place of Britain in the global economy and in the development of global markets
- concerns about environmental issues and the use of resources
- re-valuation of the place of non-teaching staff in the education process
- the pressure to achieve 'more for the same' brought about by budgetary constraints and increased emphasis on targets and performance measures.

So how should schools be responding to these challenges, and what can be done to support them?

School responses

Schools are already exploring solutions for a changing world. Some of these approaches can be broadly categorised as follows:

Increasing the emphasis on learning

Traditionally, the world of education has concentrated on teaching, making the assumption that learning will follow inevitably. However, the emphasis of the late 1980s and the 1990s on assessing and recording standards of achievement has forced a re-thinking of this simplistic view. Students' learning rather than teachers' teaching is increasingly seen to be at the crux of the education process: the emphasis has moved from inputs to outcomes.

Re-aligning teachers to be 'directors of learning'

The increasing emphasis on the process of learning has caused many schools, and teachers themselves, to review the teaching function. Teachers often now conceptualise their roles more in terms of 'directors of learning' than as purveyors of teaching. The change is a subtle one which does not deny the traditional 'art and science' of teaching; but it concentrates more on the use of those skills to bring about learning in the student.

Assessing the implications of the new technologies

Among the most powerful resources which teachers, as directors of learning, have at their disposal is the developing technology bound up in Information Technology. This opens up entirely new avenues of communication, making access to data simple, self-study a powerful tool, and availability of information international.

Extending teachers' roles to be managers of the learning environment in its widest sense

Old-fashioned concepts of 'one teacher, one class' for primary schools, or of 'one subject specialist, one class' in the secondary sector are, in the scenario we have painted, as redundant in the twenty-first century as Victorian pupil-monitors are today. The teachers of the future may exercise less of a role in class control or in the traditional skills of exposition: they may well be the programme-makers and resource creators of the future. They will not 'do the teaching', they will manage (in every sense) the intellectual environment that students will inhabit.

Reappraising patterns of learning

One of the implications of the picture painted here is that not only will teachers' roles and patterns of working change, but so will those of the learners. With more and more computers home-based, even portable, not all learning will need to take place in schools as they are currently modelled. The purposes of school buildings and their patterns of use will become subject to reappraisal.

What must we do?

Education stands at a cross-roads. One of the ways in which some educationists are dealing with this is to establish projects, such as the *Schools for the Future* project with which I have been involved at the University of Lincolnshire and Humberside. The project is primarily intended to support developments and changes for this twenty-first century world. It is attempting to do this in a number of ways, as shown below.

Through an analysis of change as it affects education

The project will be alert for, and seek out, the global and national trends in education which are likely to affect schools and learning in the immediate future.

Through research into innovative practice

In particular, the project will seek out innovative practice, large- or small-scale, in Britain and overseas. Whenever possible, we will try to explore at first hand not just the problems and their solutions, but the decision-making processes and creative approaches which have been used.

Through a specific research project on the use of school time and plant

The project team is already involved with a Funding Agency project in a group of schools in London. Here we are experimenting with one of the fundamental issues to face *Schools for the Future*: the structure of the school day and the school year. This is a collaborative venture located in three schools in which we shall be monitoring and evaluating not only the outcomes (in terms of new patterns of attendance and their effects), but also the kinds of radical thinking which are used to arrive at solutions.

Through an examination of the developing uses of new technologies in schools

One of the keys to future developments in education will, inevitably, be the uses to which new technologies are put. These are already developing as a powerful tool for communication, and to a lesser extent for learning. These parallel developments are set to continue; and the ways in which they are adopted into, and woven into the fabric of, educational provision in the future are potentially very challenging to traditional thinking about schools and their functions. The project will seek to explore both innovation in this field, and to speculate about alternative models of learning.

Through an examination of the decision-making processes and mind-sets needed to bring about dramatic change

This project is about dramatic, rather than marginal, change. In the project's studies of innovative practice we shall be as concerned with the thinking process leading to change as with the change itself. These are largely uncharted waters, and we shall be breaking new ground in exploring this issue – which may have implications for the selection and education of leaders for the future.

Through dissemination of best practice

A fundamental purpose of this project will be to pass on to the education world the lessons which we are able to learn. We shall do this through whatever channels are most appropriate: visits, courses, conferences, books, journal articles, in-service training events, the Internet and the media. Our main concern will not be to provide examples of practice which others may copy directly in their own situations, but to tease out the principles which others may apply to reach their own conclusions in their unique situations.

What are the broad philosophies behind the project?

Schools for the Future is based on the principles of reengineering. Michael Hammer defines reengineering as:

> *The fundamental rethinking and radical redesign of business processes to bring about dramatic improvements in performance."*
> **(Hammer, M and Champy, P (1997) The Reengineering Revolution Handbook. *New York: Harper Business, p3*)**

At the heart of the reengineering philosophy is the client/customer. Reengineering is about providing a better service in a changing environment; but it is more than tinkering with structures to achieve marginally more acceptable results. Reengineering uses the best insights from other management theories (team-work, total quality management, etc.), but is much more than the sum of these parts. It is a mind-set that uses creative thinking in a focused way to achieve quite different ways of working. It is anticipatory rather than reactive.

Reengineering and teaching skills

This series of books of teaching skills has developed out of my interest in reengineering as well as from my long-term involvement with the initial and in-service training of teachers. Part of the intention of the series is to identify those traditional teaching skills which will continue to be fundamental to the teacher in the twenty-first century, and to provide a means of support for those who wish to acquire or improve them. Thus class management is likely to remain a fundamental skill for teachers: but its nature will change to accommodate the new roles for teachers as directors of learning and as managers of para-professionals in the classroom. However, other skills, such as the exploitation of the new technologies, are of recent origin and will have to be assimilated by all teachers, including those who perhaps trained for a school system which operated rather differently in the recent past.

This book examines three skills — formulating lesson objectives, task-setting and differentiation — which have changed in character and prominence in recent years and are likely to continue to increase in importance. It tries to identify the fundamental principles which underly them, so that the reader can apply those principles in both traditional and non-traditional teaching and learning situations.

Education is changing rapidly; and the nature of the teacher's job is changing, too. Some people find change only negative and disturbing. This series treats change as a positive phenomenon: one which challenges and excites. Hopefully, these books do not lose sight of traditional wisdom nor of the continuing values of which the profession is rightly proud. But they do look forward in a spirit of progression and development to where schools are going rather than to where they have been.

Professor Trevor Kerry
Series Editor

How to use this book

This is a book of teaching skills for teachers of students in the middle years: Key Stages 2 and 3. It aims to equip both beginning and more experienced teachers with the skills they need to formulate learning objectives, set tasks, and differentiate work for students more effectively in their classrooms.

The text is designed to draw together the essential knowledge about the skills of formulating objectives, task-setting and differentiating based on the work of major researchers, and to present this knowledge in a way, and in a language, which is immediately accessible. Because the book consists of interactive skills, the intrusion of references in the text has been kept to a minimum. Only key references to these skills (as opposed to more general works) have been cited.

This book is designed to take the reader on from knowledge to skill by providing the text in an interactive format: there are Activities through which the components of the skills can be practised. It is suggested that the reader makes use of these Activities and thus reflects – through keeping a log, through the use of tape-recording or by being observed by a colleague – on his or her performance to reach greater levels of proficiency and understanding.

In practice, the book can be used in different ways:

- It can be read as a continuous text: the reader then simply omits the Activities as they arise.
- It can be used as a training book: the reader must pause at each Activity and undertake it at the appropriate point in the text.
- It can be used as a source book: the reader may dip into those sections which seem most pertinent at the time, treating both text and Activities selectively.

Similarly, the contexts of use may vary. The book can be used by an individual teacher working alone towards self-development. It can be used within a school, and the Activities built into in-house professional development. The book could also form the basis of school-based in-service work led by an adviser or external consultant. The material lends itself to use during teaching practices by initial trainees, or to reinforce skills during the early years of teaching. The material may also assist headteachers and others acting as appraisers to observe the formulation of learning objectives, the setting of tasks, and the process of differentiating students' work in more focused ways.

Chapter 1

What are learning objectives?

Towards a definition

Learning objectives are hedged around with unnecessary mystique. They are, quite simply, the answers to this question:

At the end of this lesson/session/term/year, what do I want my students to know, to do or to understand which will take their learning on from where it is now?

It is probably worth pausing over this definition.

Many readers will recall the laboured hours spent preparing for teaching practice, during which time you were required to write lesson notes. The most difficult section was always the bit which asked you to identify your aims and objectives for the lesson. Indeed, most people have great problems in sorting out the differences between these two items. For my own part I have a simple rule-of-thumb for distinguishing between them.

Aims: are long-term, all-embracing and tend towards the philosophical or ideal. For example, in a technology lesson on cooking, a long-term aim might be to encourage students to work safely in the kitchen (keeping hair away from flames, guarding hands from the oven with appropriate protection and so on). Every lesson would aim to teach safety (or hygiene, or high standards of presentation etc.) or to re-inforce it.

Objectives: are shorter-term, immediate and rapidly testable. So, in the cookery lesson, the immediate objective is to make an edible steak and kidney pie. This may involve learning some new skills of food preparation, or an understanding of how to make particular kinds of pastry. But the end-product is judged by its edibility, taste, look etc.

Despite these definitions, though, there is a simpler way to think about what lessons are hoping to achieve. This is to use the word **intention**.

Intention is a generic term which can cover both the aim of a lesson or series of lessons, and the objective. Intentions can be shorter-term or long-term. The long-term intentions of our cookery classes are to encourage safety in working, hygienic practice and high standards of presentation in food preparation. The short-term intentions are to enable the students to create specific dishes, or to make particular items like types of pastry.

Although this is a chapter about learning objectives, the little word intention will be a most useful one to have in mind to help cut through the jargon. It will, perhaps, help with the next point: which is that learning objectives are often divided into what are called **domains**. There are five domains which feature in this classification, but for the moment we shall look in detail at just three:

- the knowledge domain;
- the skills domain;
- the domain of understanding.

We must now look at each of these in turn to see what exactly each means in the context of a lesson.

Learning objectives in the knowledge domain

These answer the question:

At the end of this piece of work/session, what do I want the students to know that they did not know before?

Teachers spend a lot of their time in class talking: the intention of much of that talk – at least in part – is that students should know some new material at the end of this process. Part of the purpose of schooling is to impart knowledge. Indeed quite a lot of the curriculum is predicated on the assumption that, having worked their way through the syllabus of a subject or a topic, students will know certain things as a result. These things are often tested in examinations and assessments, and are typically subject to periodic feedback by teachers on progress through classroom tests.

While it could be argued that too much emphasis is placed on students acquiring factual knowledge (i.e. pieces of information – as opposed to the understanding of the implications of that information), one cannot deny that a significant intention of schooling is to teach specific pieces of knowledge: how to read; the basic number bonds; the history of Britain; what certain words mean in a modern language; the format for writing a letter; the names of the notes in a musical scale; what the scale on a map is for – and so on. Every lesson implies intentions – i.e. learning objectives – in the knowledge domain. To identify those key elements of knowledge is, in effect, to formulate the learning objectives for the lesson.

Let us take a very simple lesson. The topic is Adaptation, which comes from the Life and Living Things element of the National Curriculum in science. Our imaginary teacher begins from a visual aid: a stuffed owl. Having settled on the topic, and having acquired her visual stimulus, she now has to begin to formulate the learning objectives for the lesson. In the knowledge domain, what is she intending to achieve? Since the concept of adaptation implies knowledge of the creature's life-style (the cluster of phenomena to which it has adapted), she must be intending that the students should know about the owl's lifestyle: i.e. where and how it lives. This is the new knowledge which will flow from the lesson: so to impart this knowledge in some way must form part of the knowledge objectives of the lesson.

Our teacher may formulate a learning objective for the lesson thus:

> *At the end of the lesson (I intend that) the students will*
> *have learned some aspects of the owl's lifestyle.*

But knowledge, in itself, is not the whole story of that lesson's experience for the students. So what else forms part of the learning intentions?

Learning objectives in the skills domain

Learning objectives in the skills domain require an answer to the question:

> *At the end of this lesson/session, what do I want my students to be able to do that they could not do before?*

It might be thought, at first glance, that lessons in some subjects are more overtly skills-based than others: that design and technology lessons are more skills-related than English lessons. But that analysis will not stand scrutiny. It is fairly easy to catalogue skills across the curriculum – all of them implicit in the National Curriculum for various Key Stages. For example:

- In a geography lesson – to be able to create a map of a given area (be it the school playground or a selected piece of the outdoors).
- In a music lesson – to be able to tune an instrument.
- In a history lesson – to be able to use an index to locate information about a specific historical character.
- In an English lesson – to be able to punctuate one's own work accurately using not only full stops and commas, but also semi-colons and speech marks.
- In mathematics – to be able to look up log tables.
- In art – to be able to mix a colour to the shade required.

- In drama – to be able to control the voice to speak louder and softer, but still be heard by the audience.
- In IT – to know how to use the Edit facility.
- In science – to be able to handle acids safely.

All of these processes depend to an extent on the student's knowledge, but that knowledge has to be applied to some form of action. Students have now taken some responsibility for translating their knowledge into performance. Most lessons have skills elements embedded in them. In identifying the learning objectives of lessons, teachers need to recognise what these elements are and to formulate them appropriately in learning objectives.

So let us return to the hypothetical lesson our imaginary teacher was giving about Adaptation. She has it in mind that the students need to look hard at the stuffed owl in order to begin to work out how it lives (that it has a hooked bill for tearing flesh, for example). Observation is important in science and is a skill. She will want them to draw the owl in order to record their observations. Later – when they have learned more about the owl's digestive system, which is specially designed to cope with bone and feather – she will want the students to dissect pellets of these materials regurgitated by the owl in order to identify items in the owl's diet. The observation, the drawing and the dissection all require skills.

So the teacher might formulate some further lesson objectives:

At the end of this lesson (I intend that) the students will have observed accurately and acutely the main features of the bird.

At the end of this lesson (I intend that) the students will be able to use their observation skills to draw a reasonable representation of the bird showing its main features.

At the end of the lesson (I intend that) the students will be able to dissect an owl's pellet efficiently.

So now the students will have both a knowledge of owls which will lead them towards the concept of Adaptation, and the skills to carry out scientific work more effectively. However, they will still be lacking an important feature of classroom learning.

Learning objectives in the domain of understanding

Learning objectives in the domain of understanding answer the question:

> *What do I want my students to understand at the end of the lesson which they did not understand before?*

Knowledge without understanding is a sterile accomplishment. Long John's parrot may have been able to trot out information overheard from drunken sailors, but it would have done him no good because he didn't know how to put the information to use! In an earlier book in this series (*Questioning and Explaining in Classrooms*) considerable time was spent on looking at how explanations 'give understanding to another'. In our imaginary lesson on Adaptation, the teacher not only wants the students to acquire some facts about owls and their lifestyle, but to manipulate those facts into an appreciation of how the owl – over time – has evolved to deal with its lifestyle:

- Its head – can swivel in a wide arc in order to see prey without having to move and create noise.
- Its feet – are covered in hair to deaden the sound of its take-off prior to pouncing.
- Its wings – have specially adapted feathers which make its flight silent.
- Its talons – have evolved into stiletto sharpness for killing and holding prey.

From these observations, the link between the observed characteristics of the owl and the knowledge about its lifestyle gradually build into a picture – a conceptual map – of the relationship between form and behaviour. This conceptual map we call **understanding**.

Real learning consists of acquiring, making sense of, relating and synthesising many such conceptual maps. Moving learning on requires the teacher to build new concepts effectively and to give students the opportunity to test them and make those links.

So the teacher in our hypothetical lesson may formulate some further learning objectives, this time in the domain of understanding:

At the end of this lesson (I intend that) the students will be able to understand how observed features of the owl's anatomy have evolved to assist its lifestyle.

At the end of this lesson (I intend that) the students will have acquired a conceptual grasp of the key technical term 'Adaptation' with a view to linking it to other technical language ('evolution', an idea already introduced to the class; and others, such as habitat, to be introduced later).

Taking stock of learning objectives

This is an opportune moment to pause and take stock. In trying to illustrate how learning objectives work, we have hypothesised a lesson on Adaptation, starting from a stuffed owl, and led by a teacher who has formulated three kinds of learning objective: of knowledge, of skill and of understanding. So, if this teacher were writing down those objectives (let us say as part of the set of lesson notes which she has to produce for a visit by an Ofsted inspector), what would she put? This is what she has collected so far:

At the end of the lesson (I intend that) the students will have learned some aspects of the owl's lifestyle.

At the end of this lesson (I intend that) the students will have observed accurately and acutely the main features of the bird.

At the end of this lesson (I intend that) the students will be able to use their observation skills to draw a reasonable representation of the bird showing its main features.

At the end of the lesson (I intend that) the students will be able to dissect an owl's pellet efficiently.

At the end of this lesson (I intend that) the students will be able to understand how observed features of the owl's anatomy have evolved to assist its lifestyle

> *At the end of this lesson (I intend that) the students will have acquired a conceptual grasp of the key technical term 'adaptation' with a view to linking it to other technical language ('evolution', an idea already introduced to the class; and others, such as habitat, to be introduced later).*

This list is quite impressive, and gives a good flavour of the kind of intellectual learning which will be taking place in the lesson. The Ofsted inspector will be in no doubt, on reading the notes, what the teacher's intentions for the lesson are. Both the inspector and the teacher, in their different ways, will be able to gauge student progress against the objectives – a point to which we shall return later in the book. But the form of the objectives listed above is a bit clumsy and long-winded – many teachers would feel threatened about having to produce so much paper for one set of lesson objectives. It has been convenient for us to record them in this way in order to identify the thought processes which underpin them. Now we can begin to shorten the format. What our imaginary teacher might write could be something nearer to this:

LEARNING OBJECTIVES FOR THE LESSON:

Students will be able . . .

- *to learn some aspects of the owl's lifestyle*
- *to observe accurately and acutely the main features of the bird*
- *to use their observation skills to draw a reasonable representation of the bird showing its main features*
- *to dissect an owl's pellet efficiently*
- *to understand how observed features of the owl's anatomy have evolved to assist its lifestyle*
- *to acquire a conceptual grasp of the key technical term 'adaptation' with a view to linking it to other technical language.*

Our imaginary teacher has done quite a good job so far of generating learning objectives which are meaningful (that is, they give students real and measurable targets to achieve); which are based on sound theory (for example, they move from the concrete through the conceptual to the abstract); and which are simple to understand (so that an observer can track what is happening). Before you proceed any further in this chapter, perhaps it is time to take stock, too, of your own approach to composing learning objectives by undertaking Activity 1.

Activity 1
Exploring your own learning objectives

Find some recent lesson notes which you have made. Go through them, and pull out the learning objectives you have composed.

Do they fall into the three domains described in this chapter:

- knowledge;
- skills;
- understanding?

Are any of these domains under- or over-represented in your learning objectives?

Do any of your learning objectives appear to fall outside these three domains? In what ways?

(Keep a notebook of your responses to each Activity in this book as you come to it. This will build into a learning resource.)

The inter-relationships between learning objectives

However, you may have discovered through Activity 1 that not all learning objectives are quite as easily categorised as those which have been used as examples so far in this chapter. This is because – in formulating an objective – one often needs to mix elements from two or more of the three kinds discussed so far: knowledge, skill and understanding-related objectives. An example may help.

As the work on Adaptation unfolds, our imaginary teacher is intending to use information gleaned from the dissection of pellets. The dissection will reveal what the owl has eaten during the last few hours: probably some combination of rodents (rats, mice, voles) and various beetles. By gathering a lot of data from the class's dissection of pellets it will be possible to get some feel for the proportion of different foods eaten. This the teacher wants the students to display in the form of a pie-chart. Her learning objective is:

To turn data gained from a study of pellets into a pie-chart.

Such an objective requires a mix of abilities from the students. They must have a knowledge of how to construct pie-charts; and an understanding of how the data is to be acquired and displayed. If they use a computer to generate the chart they may need key-boarding and IT skills. This learning objective, then, crosses the domains previously identified; and the teacher needs to be aware of this.

Further domains for learning objectives – 1: the attitudinal domain

Not all learning objectives have to relate to the actual knowledge, skills and understanding which students acquire. It is equally legitimate to formulate learning objectives about the **way** in which such learning is acquired. One of the concomitants of the learning gained is the attitudes to learning which students receive through their experiences of school. Think back for a moment over your own education: what did you hate most? For many it was mathematics; and what we learned in maths was often to dislike maths more! But what if the opposite had happened?

In recent years successive political administrations have made much play of the need for teachers to teach subjects and to 'communicate a love of the subject' to their students. While it is certainly possible to argue a case that subjects are less (or at least no more) significant than the inter-relations between them, it remains true that the distinctive elements of subjects – what are often referred to as the 'disciplines' of the subject – can be a source of fascination. To pick up on this fascination is precisely the point of learning objectives in the attitudinal domain.

Such objectives could be written for the Adaptation lesson. They might include:

> *By the end of the lesson (I intend that) the students will have understood some of the mystery surrounding owls and their lifestyle... or*

> *By the end of the lesson (I intend that) the students will have discovered the fun of engaging in scientific enquiry through exploring a real problem (i.e. the dissecting of pellets exercise).*

However, the attitudinal domain is not the only other domain worthy of mention here.

Further domains for learning objectives – 2: the affective domain

Not only is the way in which students learn important, but the **context** in which that learning takes place may also be significant. In a previous book in this series (*Questioning and Explaining in Classrooms*) there was a review of some of the most influential learning theories currently recognised as useful. Among these theories was Social Constructivism. Constructivism itself suggests that students learn through the interaction of thought and experience; Social Constructivism emphasises the part played by others in that process. Social Constructivists understand that the social relations, communications and conversations between teacher and student and between student and student, all help to promote the learning which takes place. Social Constructivism highlights the role of classroom organisation for learning in enabling students to communicate freely: for example, through group work or discussion. The principles can once again be applied to the formulation of learning objectives. Thus our imaginary teacher of Adaptation might have included in her learning objectives one in the affective domain:

> *By the end of this lesson (I intend that) the students will have promoted their learning through working collaboratively in groups to dissect their pellets and collect data from the exercise.*

Collecting the learning objectives from the five domains

So we are now in a position to draw together all the learning objectives formulated in this chapter – those from the first three (cognitive) domains, and those from the latter two (process) domains. The result looks like this:

LEARNING OBJECTIVES FOR THE LESSON:

Students will be able....

- to learn some aspects of the owl's lifestyle;
- to observe accurately and acutely the main features of the bird;
- to use their observation skills to draw a reasonable representation of the bird showing its main features;
- to dissect an owl's pellet efficiently;
- to understand how observed features of the owl's anatomy have evolved to assist its lifestyle;
- to acquire a conceptual grasp of the key technical term 'Adaptation' with a view to linking it to other technical language;
- to understand some of the mystery surrounding owls and their lifestyle;
- to discover the fun of engaging in scientific enquiry through exploring a real problem (i.e. the dissecting of pellets exercise);
- to work collaboratively in groups to dissect pellets and collect data from the exercise.

This set of objectives is quite impressive, emanating as it does from a lesson, or short sequence, on the theme of Adaptation. What has emerged from the formulation of them is, hopefully, the understanding that these intentions are not bolt-ons to the lesson, but entirely integral to it. The irritation which many teachers express when faced with having to generate learning objectives is not acceptable, because the formulation of objectives should be part of a teacher's daily professionalism. What many practising teachers have failed to grasp, and what teachers in training have to learn, is how to think in intentions: to develop the mind-set that stands back from the teaching process and can analyse it objectively in this way. As professionals we are accountable, and that means being able to answer questions like:

■ Why are you teaching this material?
■ Why are you teaching it like this?
■ What are you hoping your students will achieve as a result?

Learning objectives serve this purpose for us in our daily lives.

Learning objectives: pulling together the threads

Having established what learning objectives are, and to some extent how they can be arrived at, it is time to deal with a few other insights into the learning objective process.

This chapter has suggested quite forcibly that all learning objectives have two essential components:

■ **An intention on the part of the teacher;**
■ **A learning outcome to be gained by the student.**

So, in composing learning objectives, teachers have simply to ask themselves the two key questions: what do I intend this lesson/session to achieve, and what will the students gain from it? The gains are then defined under the five domains described above (and see also Figure 1).

One difficulty which teachers tell me they have in drawing up learning objectives relates to what might be called 'the chicken and the egg' question. That is, which comes first: the lesson or the objective? In other words, should I devise my lesson and then write the objectives? Or do I write some objectives and then fit the lesson round them? The answer is much the same as the one in the chicken-and-egg conundrum! Perhaps Figure 2 will help to throw some light on the fairly subtle inter-play between these components.

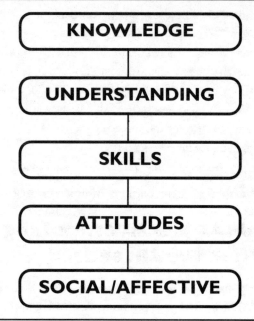

Figure 1 – *Learning objectives: the 5 domains*

The last task for you in this chapter is to review some of your own practice in establishing learning objectives in your teaching situation by tackling Activity 2.

Activity 2
Improving your own learning objectives

Look back to the learning objectives you used in Activity 1 – these were drawn from some recent lessons which you had taught.

Now try to improve on the objectives you wrote at the time, using the insights gained from this chapter.

You may add objectives to those you originally composed.

Assess the improved insights this process has given you into your own teaching.

The curriculum:
what has to be taught?

Special factors:
e.g. is it exam
work?

The students:
(age, ability range)

L E A R N I N G   O B J E C T I V E S

Relationship
of the lesson
to previous/
future work

Classroom context:
(box classroom,
specialist area etc.)

Students' previous
experience (e.g. of
whole class/group/
individualised work)

Length of time
available

Nature of the class
(well/not so well behaved;
mixed or single gender etc.)

Figure 2 – Some factors in composing learning objectives

Chapter 2

Learning objectives: some underlying issues

The nature of the problem

As I was writing this chapter I came across a very persuasive short paper by an American named O.L. Davis Jr. Davis' argument is simply this: that curriculum and teaching are intentional; they influence but do not cause learning. In recent years, especially in Britain, politicians have espoused the belief that if curriculum could be improved, then standards would rise. The result of this enterprise was the National Curriculum. Few teachers seriously believe that students necessarily perform better as a result of it, yet that was its intention. Since its intention did not seem to work particularly well, the politicians sought others: they invented schemes for 'improving' teaching, such as the 'Super Teacher' concept, and for holding up high performing or 'Beacon' schools as exemplars. Again, intentions, but as yet unproven in the scheme of things. And so, Davis concludes that much of this enterprise is futile; and in a poignant passage he describes the failure in a metaphor:

> *Remember the British experience in the trenches that snaked across northern France in the Great War. For four years, the pride of England formed in ranks, charged across no-man's land, and were mown down like grain at harvest time. . .Unfortunately, the end of the story is known. The German trenches held. . . .British valour did not cause victory simply because generals ordered or desired victory.*
>
> **(Davis, O.L., jr (1998) 'Curriculum and Teaching: no guarantees of learning' Education Today vol. 48.2 pp28-31)**

Curriculum and teaching, Davis goes on, are not consequential but intentional; they intend but cannot guarantee learning. So is learning a hopeless case? No, for Davis maintains:

> *. . . teachers must teach more mindfully in order that their actions begin to match their principled and rich intentions.*
>
> **[op.cit. p31].**

This book began by formulating learning objectives as a precursor to students' learning. Just as the British generals needed not more charges but better tactics to succeed, so for teachers – in order to translate intentions into learning – they need better skills and strategies, of which the formulation of effective learning objectives is just the beginning. As the book unfolds the relationship between learning objectives (teaching intentions) and learning outcomes will be explored. For the moment, however, let us pause over some of the ways in which learning objectives can be turned into tactics for improving learning.

The long, the medium, and the short

In practice the learning objectives which teachers formulate tend to relate to one of three time-scales:

- **long term** – things that need to be achieved through the syllabus/curriculum for the year
- **medium term** – things that need to be achieved this term
- **short term** – things that have to be achieved this week or in this lesson now

This time-scale issue is quite important. The longer-term goals tend to drive the shorter-term ones. However, longer-term goals tend to be more general: more akin to what we called, in the previous chapter, aims. By contrast, the short-term goals are more akin to what we labelled objectives. Long, medium and short-term goals are all valuable in giving both direction and purpose to learning: to setting out the intentions. Perhaps some examples of long, medium and short-term learning objectives will illustrate this:

In English, a long-term learning objective might be to encourage students to compose poetry of their own to a reasonable standard using both creative thought and an adventurous approach to form and style.

The medium-term objective for term 1 could be to expose the students to some exciting poetry: simply to capture their interest in the form, the narratives, the rhythms and the language of poetry. In term 2 the teacher might move on to the narrower learning objective of understanding how rhythms are made up through the closer, more technical examination of different types of poem: the haiku, the limerick, the epic form, and so on. By term 3 the learning objective might have shifted to students writing their own compositions based on one or more of these models.

The short-term learning objectives would relate to individual lessons. One such lesson – picked at random from a series – might be guided by the objectives that, at the end, students will be able to:

- read and enjoy the 'Smuggler's Song';
- understand the narrative;
- appreciate the rhythm;
- explain the purpose of the refrain;
- appreciate that the refrain changes connotation from verse to verse e.g. from humorous to sinister;
- make a start on preparing a narrative and rhythm of their own, prior to attempting to write to the model.

The learning objectives, regardless of time-scale, do not simply happen. All sorts of factors influence the objectives which teachers formulate;

and it is to some of these factors that we now move on in the next section of the chapter.

Factors influencing learning objectives

In the previous chapter it was suggested that a number of factors played a part in helping to determine learning objectives. These were:

- The curriculum: what has to be taught?
- The students: age, ability range.
- Special factors: e.g. is it exam work?
- Classroom context: box classroom, specialist area etc.
- Relationship of the lesson to previous/future work.
- Length of time available.
- Students' previous experience (e.g. of whole class/group/ individualised work).

These are all factors which are quite closely related to the immediate circumstances of the school, the school day and the classroom. But there are other factors – more theoretical factors or factors external to the teacher – which also influence the learning objectives teachers set.

The first group of these additional factors relates to *how* learning takes place. In formulating learning objectives teachers take into account the teaching methods which will best achieve those objectives. For example, it is hard to teach debating skills with students seated in rows listening to a lecture about them! Similarly, we hear a lot about the need of students to develop effective self-study skills; yet this is hardly achievable as an objective unless students are given tasks which allow them freedom to think for themselves. It fails if they are subjected to too much supervision. Students can't develop creative thought if what they produce has to be honed all the time to a teacher's very personal and narrow view of what constitutes excellent work. This last point may need some illustration.

Imagine a primary classroom in which students are studying World War Two. The teacher has collected some posters of the time, and found a tape of contemporary sounds like sirens, fire engines and the noise of bombing. The children listen and discuss these in a whole class setting. Then they are set to work. But the task is not only identical for each child even its parameters are highly circumscribed. They are to produce a story of a night in the Blitz under a given title. They must write between 15 and 20 lines. Their work must contain reference to each of the sounds they have heard. They are given a character around whom to hang the event. The story must contain the words: Spitfire, London and shelter. They must indicate how Londoners suffered. They are not given access to additional materials. There is to be no conferring. The end-product is to be illustrated with a picture of a plane, and the main colours are to be red and black.

Far-fetched, do you think? Not really. A bit caricatured, perhaps, and from time to time there is a case for de-limiting tasks like this. But too often both the spoken and non-verbal approval which teachers signal for classroom thinking (or lack of it) stifles creativity in otherwise quite dynamic minds.

Another influence on what kinds of learning objectives are formulated relates to the ways in which students are grouped for learning. Narrow streaming of students may influence what happens in class towards a static, desk-bound approach based substantially on listening to the teacher, followed by all students attempting an identical task. By contrast, individualising work may enable a student with a specific flair to do a task beyond the range of others in the group, yet cater simultaneously for the youngster who needs a simpler activity aided by a classroom assistant. Whole class work, group work – for example for role plays – and individualised work all have a place in learning. Matching desired outcome (the learning objective) to the appropriate grouping method will produce more effective learning as well as improving the variety of lessons and thus sustaining student interest more effectively.

The third of this cluster of issues relates to matching teaching and learning styles in the classroom. Teacher A may teach more effectively through exposition and didactic methods; teacher B may be a skilled exponent of group work. Each will tend to formulate objectives in ways which can be achieved through these methodologies. But, equally significant, students may have preferred learning styles. One may really enjoy working alone, while another may long for the anonymity of whole class activity. The crucial consideration here is balance; and by setting learning objectives such that they demand this balance from a week's, a term's or a year's work, is an important part of planning for teaching.

Activity 3

Considering a range of teaching methods

Part of the skill of the successful teacher is to vary his/her teaching methods in order to achieve the learning objectives for the lesson by using *appropriate* teaching methods.

The following is a list of some teaching methods. Think back over your last term's teaching. How often did you use each method? Add any other categories you wish to list:

Teaching method used:	often	occasionally	never
Exposition			
Questioning			
Practical work/ experiments			
Problem-solving			
Simulation			
Role play			
Practice tests			
Debate			
Team teaching			
Self-study by students			
Written exercises			
Peer critique			
Self-marking by students			
Others:			

Now scrutinise the results of this exercise. How varied is your teaching? If it falls into predictable patterns, can you suggest reasons why?

A second cluster of factors which influences the kinds of learning objectives which are set relates to the group of people whom we might call clients of the education system. These include, for example:

- Ofsted
- Parents
- Governors
- Politicians.

We need to look at each group to try to assess its influence on learning objectives.

Ofsted inspectors work to a closely delineated set of criteria for judging the effectiveness of schools. They need to be assured that all the statutory criteria for education are met, that policies and other paperwork are in place, and that school governors are overseeing the delivery of curriculum in the school. They measure students' progress and attainment; and they assess the teaching, and the response from students to that teaching. Though the official line might be that no one philosophy of education or style of delivery is favoured by Ofsted, many teachers will be suspicious of this. Indeed, it might well be true to say that individual inspectors are open on this issue, but it is hard to sustain the same argument for Her Majesty's Chief Inspector. As an individual, HMCI is frequently in print advocating specific styles of teaching which tend, if one can use jargon, to be at the formal end of the continuum. Many teachers will respond to this covert pressure by shifting their lessons and planning in this direction, at least when an inspection is likely or imminent.

Parents can have a strong influence on teachers' planning, and hence on their learning objectives. Parents of primary students may want to see evidence of 'hearing students read', or of the 'testing of tables'. They may be quite hostile to legitimate educational activities, the value of which they do not understand but which can be labelled 'play' or 'topic work' or whatever they have been conditioned to believe is the bogey of the educational system at that moment. Similarly, parents of students moving towards GCSE/GCE examinations will, naturally, be concerned about results and may blame the methods of teaching if the results do not match their own expectations.

School governors play a similar role in a different forum. Since, in the post-Thatcherite market economy (which remains unreversed under New Labour) schools now have to compete for students and recruit against the threat of closure, governors want to see results too. Again, teachers may feel constrained to limit their teaching methods and cram students for examinations or assessments simply to satisfy their governing bodies.

Much of this pressure itself comes, ultimately, from politicians. One could argue that it is a bad thing when politicians take no interest in education: the financial and other provision tends to lessen. One could argue. too, that it is a worse thing when they do take an interest: they tend to set up agendas which are more political and less educational! The stress of this situation was well summarised recently by Karen Thornton in an article in the *Times Educational Supplement*:

> *A curious mixture of pragmatism and idealism characterises the work of the Government group charged with finding, disseminating and implementing good teaching practice. Pragmatism, because the members want to produce practical and effective guidance for schools. Idealism, because they see the key to the whole process in the more esoteric area of tapping teachers' own creativity, boosting professional confidence and status, and encouraging reflective practice. The tensions thrown up by these two approaches. . .look set to keep the nine-strong team busy for some time to come.*
> **('In search of excellence' TES, 15.5.98 p20)**

The simple truth is that one can't have a reflective profession, learning from its own action-based research and development, when there is strong external pressure from the political masters of the system to follow a specific dogma and adopt 'preferred' procedures.

So one set of factors influencing the formulation of learning objectives relates to educational issues such as the use of appropriate teaching methods, intelligent grouping strategies, and varied teaching/learning styles. Another set of factors is that relating to satisfying the various and varied 'clients' of the education system. A third set of factors relates to the 'customers' of the system: the students.

Students themselves have views about how their education should proceed: perhaps the older the students the more articulate they can become about expressing these views. However, even young children can reflect on their own learning and how they learn best: what is known as metacognition. The very best teachers try to get their students to articulate how **they** think they learn effectively, and will use this data in formulating their learning objectives for lessons.

You can see from the argument of this section of the book that formulating learning objectives is not an easy task, nor is it one to which no pre-conceptions are brought. In the Editorial it was suggested that this volume, like others in the series, aims to equip teachers with skills for 'schools for the future'. Such schools will be increasingly subject to the kinds of external pressures described here: and the skill of unmasking those pressures and dealing with them professionally will become increasingly important.

So what has this chapter told us so far about learning objectives and their formulation? Perhaps we could summarise it thus:

- Learning objectives are 'intentional' – they don't guarantee learning will take place.
- There are many educational and non-educational pressures which operate on teachers when they try to set learning objectives.
- Nevertheless, learning objectives are important: without intentions there can be no consequences.
- The nature of the intentions (or learning objectives) has a significant influence on the consequences: i.e. whether learning takes place effectively.

So how are the consequences to be realised?

Effective planning

Formulating lesson plans is part of the larger planning process through which all teachers must go in order to teach effectively. Ofsted inspectors still claim that too few lessons are planned effectively. Yet planning is not such a difficult process. Many effective planners use a proforma of some kind to guide their thoughts. Figure 3 offers one

Date: *Class:*

Subject:

Lesson objectives (knowledge, skills, understanding, attitudinal, affective)

At the end of this session the students will be able to:

1

2

3

4

5

Outlines of content & sequence

Relationship with other learning

Materials & resources

Teaching and learning methods

Tasks to be set / methods of differentiation

Student assessment

Lesson evaluation

Figure 3 – Lesson planning proforma

such proforma – not as an exemplar, but simply as an aid for anyone without a preferred system. The advantage of the proforma in Figure 3 is that it helps the teacher to articulate carefully the learning objectives for the lesson.

The traditional classroom planning cycle looks like that in Figure 4, and many teachers will be familiar with this. However, for the present purpose an additional dimension has been added: the place of learning objectives (LOs) as central to what happens in the cycle. Learning objectives feed into and out of the cycle at every step. They inform the planning and preparation stage of a lesson. Hopefully, when the lesson is presented, the learning objectives will be implemented. Whether they have been or not will become clear at the assessment stage (whether that is informal assessment through teacher questions and feedback, or whether it is more formal measuring of learning through testing of some kind). Then the results of the assessment will feed into and inform the planning stage for the next lesson, will alter how material is presented, and so on.

Figure 4 – Teachers must not lose track of the planning cycle

Coming to terms with personal bias

This chapter has been about the influences which can operate on the formulation of learning objectives. We have looked at this topic as a precursor to translating effective learning objectives, through good preparation, into effective learning. Yet there is still one further influence which has to be revealed and recognised: the personal bias of the teacher.

The kinds of learning objectives which you set will depend upon a number of very personal issues, among the most important of which are:

- your view of curriculum theory;
- your philosophy of education;
- your preferred teaching style.

The last item has been touched on already in this chapter; so here we shall concentrate on the first two items listed. The argument runs like this:

- Your biases will subconsciously determine the nature of the learning objectives you set and ways in which you try to achieve them.
- Recognising your personal bias will help to free you from too closed a view of your intentions for your students' learning.
- Therefore, finding a way to explore your biases is important.

In this book, the way chosen to explore bias is to ask you to complete Activity 4.

Activity 4
Recognising your personal biases
Below this Activity box you will find a series of statements. Be honest, and cover all except the first one. Now read this first statement, and try to assess the extent to which you agree with it, or why you disagree.

Once you have had this 'internal debate' with yourself, uncover
statement 2, and do the same thing again.

Repeat the process one statement at a time.

Assess your own biases towards the educational process based on
this exercise. How do they condition your teaching behaviour?

Taken in isolation, each individual statement here would be
acceptable to many teachers: how tolerant would you be of those
holding each of these views?

At the end of this exercise you should have articulated to yourself
something of your beliefs and values in relation to your professional
role as a teacher.

Statements relating to Activity 4: exploring bias

Education	**is a good thing**

Education	**should include moral learning**

Education	**is best located in schools**

Education	**is ultimately a vocational activity**

Education	**in Britain should be dominated by a Christian ethos**

Education	**is incomplete without an introduction to politics**

Education	**opens minds to change**

Education	**opens doors to discontentment.**

Chapter 3

Learning objectives in practice

Some pre-requisites

Let us take stock for a moment of what we have suggested so far about learning objectives. They are the intentions for learning which teachers have for students at the end of a lesson, session or longer period of work. They can be influenced by a range of in-school and external factors. In themselves, they form no guarantee that the learning outcomes will be achieved; but, through more general lesson planning, they are a step on the road to achieving these desired outcomes. In this chapter we begin to look at how they can be operationalised.

In practice, there are three pre-conditions which are required before good learning objectives can be formulated, and before the teacher's intentions for learning can be achieved. One could argue that, in schools for the future, these three items have to become the watchwords of good professional practice. They are:

- a climate of psychological security;
- a climate which values intellect;
- a climate which encourages debate.

Let us examine each of these propositions in turn.

The first thing to say is that learning objectives – poorly constructed – can be purely mechanistic. They can consist of items like:

students will be able to:

- recite the rules for. . .
- list the dates of . . .
- recall the story about. . . and so on.

So let me declare a bias here (refer back to Activity 4). We have established in Chapter 1 that learning is not on a par with what Long John's parrot could do. It involves processes beyond the mindless stimulus-response of trotting out 'correct' answers. It demands that students **think**. However, thinking is a dangerous process. For one thing, one can think 'wrong' answers. An important part of thinking is speculation, and this may lead to the 'step in the dark' which may prove to be incorrect. How will the teacher react to this? Sadly, there does appear to be on the political agenda a view of teaching and learning which suggests that *learning right answers* is more important than thinking out – despite a few false starts – *really insightful answers* for one's self. Such a view has missed something vital.

Regurgitation is a low-level exercise: the real skill is to break new ground. But breaking new ground may meet a hostile response from a teacher paranoid about getting on and getting things 'implanted' in students' minds, especially in a climate of assessment. For a student to be willing to engage in a genuinely cognitive process he or she has to feel totally secure that the teacher will react positively, even to well-thought-out errors. That is what is meant here by psychological security.

The second point – that intellect has to be valued – relates quite closely to the first. Thinking things out – cerebration, to use a technical term – is rarely high on society's agenda of desirable characteristics.

Today's icons are hardly the intellectual elite! Sing a song with pointless words, kick a round collection of leather panels into a piece of net strung between two bits of wood, or sit in front of a goldfish bowl making ambiguous and pointless predictions in a silly voice about winners in a game of chance ('Today's lucky winner will have connections to a blue shirt !') and you can rise to fame and fortune. Invent something to improve all our lives and no-one will ever hear your name. That is the agenda of society. So it can be no wonder to us that those of our students with enquiring minds try to hide the fact – too often for fear of reprisals out of class; nor that the majority of the male student population thinks that 'it's naff to be a boff'. Teachers have to rescue society from this abyss: no-one else will. Certainly politicians won't, because it is cool to be seen with icons: some of their glory may spill onto your voting papers. But real learning can take place only in a climate which acknowledges intellect, which accepts and celebrates it and its achievements. The ethos of the school and of your own classroom is critical.

The third point is that learning objectives can be achieved only in a climate which encourages debate. This is the natural outcome of the first two. Intellect has to be traded in order to grow. Students have to be free to express their cerebration; they have to engage in debate not only with other students but with the teacher: and to do it on equal terms – that is, to know that they may sometimes lose the argument and sometimes win it. We're not, of course, talking here about questioning the teacher's authority or the school rules. We are dealing with the intellectual content of the material being taught; and – surprise though it may be to some of the population – there may be fewer 'right' answers than one is sometimes led to believe. Indeed, one could go as far as to suggest that an over-conviction of rightness stands behind most conflict in the world. This is not to suggest there are no absolute or universally desirable values; only that many conflicting groups claim to have exclusive use of them! Dogma has to be replaced by intellect wherever it occurs (and however strongly one would like to agree with it!).

Activity 5

Coming to terms with your own classroom climate

Tape-record one of your own lessons.

Later, play over the tape and try to assess the extent to which you create an appropriate climate for effective learning.

Use the criteria described in the chapter as a guide:

- Do you create an atmosphere of psychological security?
- Do you signal that you value intellectual activity?
- Do you encourage debate (teacher-student; student-student)?

What could you do to improve your performance on these criteria? Establish a plan for working on any weaknesses which this exercise has revealed.

You may feel that this section of the book has proved to be a controversial one on many levels. Perhaps the argument can be summed up like this:

- To achieve real learning outcomes in classrooms, there can be no ambiguity about whether students are required to speculate.
- To this end teachers need to question students rigorously – and students must not find this intellectual challenge threatening.
- Students' contributions have to be valued – not only by the teacher but by other students.
- Teachers have a duty to recognise that student achievements in knowledge, skills and understanding must go beyond formal assessments (SATs, GCSEs) and not be limited by them.

Turning learning objectives into criteria for learning outcomes

In the previous section it was suggested that for learning objectives to be achieved there needed to be a climate of learning which was characterised by the value placed on intellect or thinking. Within this climate students will learn effectively. To track whether the learning

Weekly planning: activities, aims, organisation

w/c 14.4

Mon: Training day – mathematics; Weds – governors' meeting
Thurs: field trip to Lincoln; Fri: contact SEN service re Tracey

English	On-going: handwriting, spelling, quiet reading Writing: to help the students record events effectively 'The most interesting event of the Easter holiday' Reading: (older, better readers) to sustain concentration
Maths	Gp 1: Rounding to nearest 10; estimating – worksheet 41 To work in pairs quietly and compare results Gp 2: Calculator work based on Nelson scheme To carry out simple operations accurately; to check by other means Gp 3: Money maths page 43; extension sheets for more able To work accurately setting out examples correctly All: mental arithmetic – To increase speed/confidence
Science	Continue tadpole diary To observe closely and draw accurately
History Geog.	Visit to Lincoln (from this very rural environment) To be prepared for the urban scene To be able to record observations using check-sheet
Art/Music	Visit to Usher Art gallery, Lincoln as part of field trip To sketch cathedral using examples in gallery as a source of ideas about style Composing a piece to create the atmosphere of the city To decide on appropriate instruments and the kind of sounds one would want to use to make 'city music'
RE	Use the visit to the cathedral to think about calmness To encourage students to articulate the idea of calmness through discussion during the cathedral visit
DT/IT	Continue work on their 'concept cars' To solve construction problems as they arise
PE	In PE – passing and catching balls, various sizes, types To improve co-ordination In swimming – revision of crawl stroke To improve confidence and skill

Figure 5 – Teacher's Planning Sheet

w/c 14.4	**Weekly evaluation**
English	Change of plans within school timetable, so handwriting transferred to next week. Reading, very quiet, purposeful The recording task – focused on a single event – did produce some quality writing. Curt made particular progress by using good detail and excellent description. Some effective discussion came from this activity – creative ideas from Sam, Jason and Tammy.
Maths	Numeracy/mental work for all: an increasing confidence, though some (esp. Greg) still rather slow Gp 1: Curt, Tracey struggled with estimating, most others secure in the concept Gp 2: Enjoyment in calculator work high. Understanding good overall. They understand the need to check. Jane said: You need to check because you might press a wrong button without noticing and get a silly answer Gp 3: Better as an activity perhaps, using the Shop Tessa understands but is struggling to set sums out tidily enough, so gets confused
Science	A lot of awe and wonder in observing the pond Excellent detail in drawings so we made a collage of them
History Geog.	Students well prepared for urban landscape, but the traffic tally proved difficult – they are insecure in a noisy situation – will try this activity in a different location Use of check-sheet to record buildings seen was done well by everyone, so we have some data to take back to school
Art/Music	Drawing the cathedral captured their interest; various styles chosen. Terri, Gail and Nick produced outstanding views City music was popular – Jason a bit silly with the drums! However, Will put together really good rhythms for assembly
RE	Sense of awe readily described by the students
DT/IT	Students made their own links between 'concept cars' and the City visit – Ben modified his design to take up less space in the crowded streets, and we were all able to discuss this
PE	Catching is improving for most except Julie; Jason has excellent co-ordination. Swimming cancelled: bus failed to arrive – objectives transferred to next session.

Figure 6 – Teacher's Evaluation Sheet

Subject:	Maths – the weather Y5,6
	NC area – handling data
Date:	17.5 – 19.5

INTENTIONS (Concepts, skills, understanding, attitudes, affective domain)
At the end of the lessons students will be able to:
1. Understand that weather varies across the country/world
2. Use maths to study weather phenomena/data
3. Understand and read block graphs with confidence
4. Solve simple problems using skills learned, in sequence
5. Enjoy the experience and relate positively to it
6. Work alone with confidence

OUTLINE OF CONTENT & SEQUENCE
Slides and photographs: Fenland, Lake District, Fuerteventura
Discuss differences; draw out possible reasons for these
Introduction to block graphs, with examples
Use specially prepared weather booklet to practise skills and set problems

RELATIONSHIP TO OTHER LEARNING
Links with geography topic work: places
Students have been collecting their own weather data from instruments in school grounds
Links to previous work in maths on 'mean' and 'modal'

MATERIALS AND RESOURCES
Special booklet
photos and slides
slide projector; also whiteboard and pens

TEACHING AND LEARNING METHODS
Observation – Group work
Questioning – whole class
Didactic – (explanation: use of block graphs)
Individual work: use of workbook

TASKS/DIFFERENTIATION
Use of workbook
Differentiation by outcome: examples are graded so most able will get further

STUDENT ASSESSMENT
To show facility with block graphs; to understand how to retrieve data and express it

LESSON EVALUATION
Lesson sequence enjoyed by all pupils
Most understood the block graph – one or two struggled: Angel, Dick
Many more than I guessed went onto the most complicated examples: esp. Terri, James, Dawn, Hannah. Rod and Denise found the early work too easy.
For some, computational skills let them down though concept understood (Terri, Dawn)
One mum told me her son had demanded the family visit Fuerteventura.

Figure 7 – Lesson plan: Weather

objectives, formulated using the five domains and the various teaching skills articulated in Chapter 1, are being achieved the scene has to shift from simply planning lessons to their implementation. In order to do this we can look at some approaches to 'planning plus implementation' based on the work of real teachers. The first example is of medium-term planning (i.e. weekly planning in this case) by a primary teacher and looks at learning objectives mainly from the teacher's perspective.

Figure 5 shows the teacher's planning sheet for the week, which includes her main learning objectives.

Figure 6 is the teacher's own assessment of where she believes the students have reached at the end of the week.

In practice these two Figures are two sides of one A4 sheet which the teacher uses to track her own (and the students') progress. Side one (Figure 5) records her intentions, side two (Figure 6) her assessment of the outcomes. Over time, this kind of recording builds into quite a significant dossier of student learning outcomes.

Of course, each individual lesson (or related sequence of lessons) is planned too. Each lesson plan has its individual learning objectives. Figure 7 shows a lesson plan for a lesson on Weather for a mixed group of students in Key Stage 2. The plan follows the format of the kind described in Chapter 2, and it includes the teacher's evaluation of the extent to which the learning objectives were achieved.

The examples show how learning objectives can be built into lesson planning, but how they can then be used to guide the delivery and implementation of the lesson and, finally, to assess the achievement of the lesson. In this way the intentions are translated into outcomes.

Learning objectives in the assessment of teaching

Earlier it was noted that one of the areas upon which Ofsted inspectors comment, and concentrate, is teaching. In the current system, teachers are graded and their grades fed back to them as part of the follow-up to inspection. It is legitimate to ask, therefore, how learning objectives are viewed by Ofsted. The answer is more cryptic than the question. The source of evidence has to be the Framework for Inspection documents for primary and secondary schools (1995); and these yield few direct clues. My reading of them, however, suggests the following.

Ofsted expects that 'there should be clear evidence of programmes of study in the classroom work observed'. So teachers, in their lesson notes, need to articulate those links. The Framework documents also indicate that inspectors expect that 'students are able to cover the required material in appropriate depth'. This statement is content-led and begs a number of the cognitive questions of the kind discussed in the previous chapter.

An important criterion for Ofsted is whether there is 'continuity and progression'. The argument here is that, if learning objectives are clearly formulated, and if they can be seen to be translated into learning, there is clear evidence of continuity and progression for the students.

Ofsted looks for a 'whole school' approach with 'learning outcomes monitored by senior staff' – a statement which suggests that (though valuable when adopted by individual teachers) the learning objective approach suggested in this book would be valuable for whole schools to adopt as part of their teaching and learning policy.

On knowledge, understanding and skills, there is within Ofsted the expectation that 'teaching methods and organisational strategies are employed to achieve stated goals'. One would argue here that the stated goals certainly include learning objectives for the short, medium and longer terms; and that this statement supports the view expressed in Chapter 2: that teaching methods and issues related to grouping and teaching style dealt with earlier (see page 21) are indeed assessed during inspection.

Ofsted also look for:

- careful assessment based on regular observations;
- whether formal records to be kept;
- equality of access and opportunity.

Each of these issues is or can be dealt with, in part at least, through setting appropriate learning objectives; and the material in Figures 5, 6 and 7 illustrate acceptable ways of documenting that these things are happening consistently (i.e. whether there is an inspection going on in the school or not).

Finally, Ofsted states that 'what is taught' is more significant that 'what is documented'. Most teachers would be sceptical of this declaration. On a lesson by lesson basis, inspectors **do** look for documented evidence of what is taught and criticise any lack in this area. The teacher who leaves to chance whether an individual inspector can deduce the learning objectives of a lesson without documentation is playing Russian roulette!

So, while the guidance is small and often unclear, there are enough clues here to say that the formulating of learning objectives, combined with evidence of their delivery and the monitoring of their success, will be a valuable asset in an inspection.

Using learning objectives in recording achievement

So far, the emphasis in discussing learning objectives has been on their formulation in the planning process, and then on their delivery in the teaching of a lesson or sequence of lessons. There has been some mention of their use in evaluating the success of lessons by the teacher: both self-evaluation and external evaluation. Now the time has come to shift the emphasis to their role in recording outcomes for students.

Record-keeping can be a sensitive topic for teachers. The increase in paperwork and meetings over recent years is a bone of contention in the profession. However, the issue of recording has to be grasped.

All teachers, as part of their professional activity, have to record the work and progress of students: from nursery to PhD level this is *sine qua non* of the business of teaching. No teaching can be effective unless the teacher understands the prior achievements of the learners: and the widely-claimed 'instinct' and 'gut-feeling' are not professional concepts (least of all in an age of accountability). Exactly when recording is done is an issue for school managements and for teacher unions. Let it simply be stated here that there is, and can be, no escape from the process if teaching is to be credible. So what are some of the issues which cling to the business of making those inevitable records?

In my own view there are five key questions which have to be answered for any kind of record keeping:

- What to record?
- How to record it?
- Where to record it?
- For what audiences?
- How often?

These are issues which have to be on the agenda of school management and staff meetings. There are statutory obligations to be met; and there are issues about in-school accountability too, for example of teachers to heads of department, to headteachers, to parents and – perhaps most importantly – to students.

In addition to these issues, there are issues of evaluation and review: and these are internal school issues. They can be summed up like this:

- Teachers need systems with which to review their own practice.
- Faculties/departments/year groups need to review their collective practice, too.
- The data on which these reviews take place need to be both qualitative and quantitative.

What does all this mean?

Recording student progress

At the level of the classroom, there have to be in place recording systems which tell the teacher and the student how students are performing. At the simplest, such a system consists of some form of marking/grading of on-going work, the results being recorded in a mark-book. This was the warp and weft of professional activity for many years: so long as there was a string of marks for each student/class each term, everyone was happy. Only rarely were questions asked about the significance of the marks, i.e. what they actually meant, or indeed what they represented in learning terms.

But what are the alternatives? On the level of recording as a process, the whole thing can be made to look more sophisticated these days by putting the data onto computer: but this does not guarantee increased meaningfulness!

The simple truth is that we all need to look more carefully at a variety of assessment techniques, so that what we record has real meaning in terms of the thinking students are asked to do. If, as many teachers claim to believe, SATs are inadequate because they measure only a limited amount of what is learned in the classroom, and they are mechanistic in their operation, then the profession has to come up with alternatives to supplement in-school recording and compensate for the inadequacies of SATs. To this end, you might like to try Activity 6.

Activity 6
Evaluating assessment methods
Below is a list of just some of the more usual and unusual methods of assessing student work.
In each case undertake an analysis of the advantages and the disadvantages of the method. Try to find at least three advantages and three disadvantages for each method. Add any methods of your own not listed here.
When you have done this, look over the result. Make a judgement about an appropriate situation in which to use each of the methods.
Try out your conclusions in your own classes.

Method	Advantages	Disadvantages	Used most appropriately to...
Teacher marks set work			
Self-assessment by students			
Peer assessment (students mark each other's work)			
Periodic tutorial review			
Personal target setting			
Students use reflective log: (What I have learned this week...)			
Other methods:			

The Activity has, hopefully, focused your mind on the fact that a range of assessment methods can be used, all of them productively in appropriate circumstances, and that most teachers could broaden their range of assessment techniques. But assessment has to be set against criteria: and those criteria have to include or relate to the learning objectives which have been set for the lesson/session/term etc. This can be illustrated by looking at a single assignment set to students, to explore how the process works.

An example of learning objectives linked to a student assignment: using pre-agreed criteria for assessment

The next point is an important one: many teachers do set learning objectives for lessons – but they miss out on a vital step in the process. They forget to tell the students what they are!

Achieving learning objectives is best accomplished through a partnership between teachers and students. This can mean that, at the beginning of a lesson, the teacher spells out the objectives which it is hoped will be achieved by the end. In relation to a specific piece of work, these learning objectives can be set down as criteria. The criteria then become, effectively, the 'marking grid' against which the work is judged.

Figure 8 sets out one such task set to students in which the learning objectives have been converted into criteria for judging the work.

The task:

For many ordinary people in Victorian England life was sordid, dangerous and uncomfortable. Yet one book on the period was called 'The Victorian Achievement'.

What exactly were the achievements of the Victorian era? How significant have they been in shaping later events?

Criteria
1. You must show a knowledge of the period and its aftermath.
2. You must have a coherent 'thesis' or line of argument.
3. You must weigh evidence about the importance of people/events etc.
4. You must make reasoned judgements.
5. Your English should be readable and persuasive.

Figure 8 – An example of pre-agreed criteria for an assignment in history

Activity 7

Turning learning objectives into criteria for judging students' work

Examine the example set out in Figure 8.

If this is a technique which you do not use already, prepare some work for students in which you use this technique to supply them with a clear set of task instructions that includes the criteria for judgement.

Allow students to complete the task. Assess their performance. Did the technique help them to focus their responses to the task set? Did they do better than you might have expected? In what ways? If not, why not?

Metacognition

It would be wrong to leave the topic of student assessment against learning objectives without some reference to metacognition. This is a rather high-sounding term for the process whereby students reflect on their own learning: *what* they have learned and the *processes* by which they learned it.

This is a technique which I have seen used effectively with students as young as Year 1 – so it is definitely appropriate for all the students whose performance is covered by this volume. But, it does require a bit of explanation from the teacher, and some training of students to help them to do it well.

At Key Stages 2 and 3 students can write adequately, so the best approach is for them to keep a written log. The teacher simply puts aside about 12 to 15 minutes a week for the log to be completed (it can be homework time rather than class time).

The teacher first explains that people learn better when they are conscious of learning. So students are invited to reflect on the week's learning. They can begin from quite easy questions (these can be duplicated and pasted into the front of the logs as reminders):

- What learning did I enjoy most this week? Why?
- What learning did I least enjoy? Why?
- What is it that I find difficult about some topics?
- What kinds of teaching help me to learn best?

They can then proceed to more difficult issues:

- What patterns of study help me learn best?
- How do I remember things most effectively?
- What targets do I need to set myself for the next week/term?
- How well did I achieve last week's targets?

Over time, students' responses to this task become more insightful, and therefore more valuable to them and to the teacher. Consider these two responses to completing a log, and you can track the process at work:

Example 1: Year 4 student, new to the process

> I liked the work we did on Greeks. It was interesting. I did not like maths. It's boring. I like story lessons.

Example 2: Year 6 students, with experience of keeping the log

> I enjoyed pretending to be a Roman soldier and the dressing up. I would have been good at bossing people about. I was afraid the new maths we did was going to be hard because it was called algebra. But it was like a game really, just finding the missing clue – good fun. I like learning things in groups like that best, and I have got less scared about maths so I do it better. I need to write neater because the numbers sometimes get jumbled.

Example 3: Year 9 student, with experience of the log

> This new history topic is really difficult because it asks you to collect your own information. I have had to give up one day's football after school to go to the Library. I can do my other homework with radio 1 on in the background. But this history I have to have silence for — so I got up very early and did it before anyone was awake. It was worth it — I got a B plus.
>
> Last week's target was to memorise the order of the battles: very hard! But Mr Smith taught me how to use a mnemonic and now I can do it.

Metacognition and the teacher

The value of this process does not stop at the student: the reflective learning log gives the teacher vital clues about what is happening in students' heads. Regular review by the teacher of what students have written in their logs is crucial. In a study of metacognition in a primary class Wilding concludes:

> *Developing metacognition is a key element in maximising children's learning. However, it is an equally important element in maximising teachers' own professionalism and quality of pedagogy — teachers need to be aware of the processes of thought that underpin their classroom practice if they are to be in control of it . . .*

and she goes on, teachers have to ask themselves, through this process:

> *Is what I am doing related to what I wanted to achieve? Are the children learning what I intended? How do the children respond to the activity? Is it justifiable as an effective way of achieving my learning aims?*
>
> **(Wilding M. (1997) 'Taking control: from theory into practice', Education Today 47.3. p23)**

So once again, learning objectives appear at the very centre of the learning process both guiding the students' achievement and revealing the teacher's effectiveness.

Chapter 4

The nature of classroom tasks

Defining classroom tasks

In the first three chapters of this book we have looked at the formulation of learning objectives. The point was made that these are achieved through what the teacher goes on to teach or asks the students to learn. They can be achieved through the materials the teacher presents verbally (explaining), through the things the teacher asks (questioning), or through the work the teacher asks the student to do (task-setting). The first two of these skill areas have been dealt with in a previous manual in this series. Here the emphasis shifts onto the third skill: that of task setting.

What exactly are classroom tasks?

My own definition of a classroom task is anything a teacher asks a student to do in order to promote learning. Some examples make the point:

- In English – to compose a letter seeking a job interview.
- In mathematics – to undertake a page of examples.
- In science – to conduct an experiment.
- In history – to collect evidence from several sources.

- In geography – to find the way round an orienteering course.
- In drama – to participate in a role play.
- In RE/DT – to model a biblical house.
- In PE – to gain a new skill in athletics.
- In IT – to operate an unfamiliar programme.

The fact is that – in class, or for homework to bring back to class – all teachers set an array of tasks every week; and all students are on the receiving end of a battery of different kinds of task every week. The purpose of the next four chapters is to give you the opportunity to reflect on the process of task setting with a view to improving this aspect of your work.

What kinds of task do teachers set?

The list above has answered this question at a superficial level. But in this section I want to explore the issue more deeply.

In a previous book in this series I argued that teachers spend a lot of time talking and asking questions. It was suggested that the intellectual demand of these activities was variable: another way of expressing this might be to say that these processes had a variable ability to promote meaningful learning objectives. The argument went on to say that improvement in the quality and intellectual demand of teachers' explanations and questions would improve learning for all students: it would raise the intellectual climate of the classroom. The same argument applies to classroom tasks.

To explore this issue further I carried out an extensive piece of classroom research some years ago. Since then I have revisited this research periodically to see whether things have changed. Frankly, they haven't! So it seems appropriate to discuss some of the insights into tasks and task-setting which were gained from this research.

What research can tell us about tasks

The problem I and my researchers set ourselves was to try to discover what kinds of intellectual demands were made by the tasks which teachers set to students. Our contention was that, if learning is fundamentally about the quality of thinking and understanding which students engage in, then the tasks teachers set should reflect that cognitive demand. To establish the extent to which this situation applied in the early years of secondary schooling we picked a number of schools at random and sat in on lessons across a range of subject areas. Later we extended the research by gathering data from the primary sector, and from a wider range of school types. From this experience we were able to develop a huge collection of task descriptions (along with examples of the ways in which students responded to the tasks). These task descriptions were then scrutinised to see whether they fell into any patterns and, if so, what those patterns were. We found we could classify classroom tasks under some fairly clearly defined headings.

The first broad categorisation was quite straightforward:

- Low order tasks
- Higher order tasks.

These labels refer to the amount of thinking, or cognitive demand, the tasks made. Let us look at some examples.

A typical low order task would be:

> When you write in your notebooks I like you to have a margin on each page. So that you don't forget, we are going to spend the next ten minutes going through notebooks so that you can draw the margins on now – on every page.

By contrast, a higher order task might be:

> Over the last couple of weeks we have read a number of short stories together, and you have done some analysis of what you think makes them effective. Now it is your chance to use that analysis to write a short story of your own . . .

Clearly, one of these tasks is more demanding than the other in terms of students' intellectual engagement. An objector might interrupt here, though, and say that the basic manual chores of classroom life have to be carried out. This is true: but they take up learning time. So – without putting ideal figures on teacher performance – a general conclusion might be that the greater the proportion of higher order tasks to low order tasks, the more learning might be happening in that specific classroom. In assessing task demand this quite simple dichotomy is really a very useful tool. Activity 8 asks you to do just that for some recent tasks you have set your own students.

Activity 8

Assessing the cognitive demand of your classroom tasks

Look back over the tasks you have set to students over the last term.

Use a simple grid to classify these into higher order (H) or low order (L):

Task	H	L
Tables test		✓
Imaginative poem	✓	
(and so on)		
Total	x	y

Now take stock of the result – a percentage measure is quite useful: number of higher order tasks x 100 divided by the total of all tasks, or 100x over x + y.

What does this exercise tell you about your own task-setting behaviour?

The results of this exercise are actually very crude, for reasons which we shall go on to explore.

Refining task definitions

One of the reasons why your analysis of task-setting in Activity 8 may be crude is that it is probably incomplete. If you looked back over students' written work, for example, you may have missed a lot of other tasks which you set during lessons for which there was no record. For our researchers, this situation did not apply. They sat in on lessons and recorded every task as it happened, so none was missed. The picture which emerged from this exercise was a complete one. This latter methodology probably picks up more of the low order tasks, and these proved to be enormously varied in nature. Table 1 sets out the variety of low level tasks which were noted – all of them more than once – and which were formed into sub-categories of low order task-setting.

Table 1

Sub-categories of low order tasks set in classrooms

Sub-category	Description
L1 Disciplinary	*Given as punishment: e.g. do extra work at break*
L2 Administrative	*Moving classroom furniture; running errands*
L3 Drawing or colouring	*Colouring in photocopied worksheets*
L4 Copying	*Usually notes from board*
L5 Reading aloud	*Usually around the class – level of engagement with material is ambiguous*
L6 Silent reading or watching	*Reading to one's self, watching a video etc. Again, engagement ambiguous, but students often seen to be off-task*
L7 Memorising	*E.g. learning lists of dates*
L8 Revising or taking revision test	*E.g. spelling tests of pre-learned words*
L9 Carrying out an experiment	*If students merely repeated something demonstrated beforehand*
L10 Simple comprehension	*E.g. hear a story or historical event, then fill in missing words in worksheet*
L11 Reinforcing	*Repeating a skill already learned: e.g. in maths, learning a new skill and initial use of it = higher level, but after 250th example becomes low order, i.e. revision*
L12 Looking things up	*Category 12 was used to described looking up simple factual information; if the data was then used (not merely collected) this would transfer to higher order.*

So, low level tasks tend to be about repeating old ground, about activities which are highly mechanistic, or they relate to work which is not designed to promote learning.

Of course, some will say that these processes have value – and they may. Planning for a shy student to carry out an errand (type L2), with a view to improving confidence, may have a value in the affective domain; but more often such tasks are unplanned and without intended purpose. Similarly it could be argued that less able students especially need to repeat work; and there is some truth in this. So while there is no absolute value judgement here, it is suggested that – as in Activity 8 – an eye needs to be kept on the erosiveness of low level activities in classrooms and the negative effects this may have on students' excitement with learning.

If these are the low level tasks, we must pursue the question: what constitutes a higher order task? For this it may be helpful to look at how to categorise students' thinking skills. Such an attempt exists in the work of Benjamin Bloom. Bloom (1956) talked about high and low order thinking skills, just as we did (above). He was able to distinguish between those operations which required a minimal level of intellectual activity to achieve, and those which provoked depth of thought and understanding. In this context, 'rewarding' a student who has just got ten sums right with the task of carrying out another twenty almost identical calculations would engage the student in lower order thinking (practice, re-inforcement). But to ask the student to take the learned skill and apply it to a new situation ('You have found the area of some of these rectangles; using squared paper can you find how to work out the area of this circle?) would be to require higher order thinking (in this case, application).

Bloom used this kind of argument to identify categories of higher order skills, not so much into a hierarchy as into different types of process. The classification which was used in the research already referred to in this chapter drew on, but adapted, Bloom's work. Table 2 lists types of higher order task, and gives examples or descriptions of them.

Table 2

Sub-categories of higher order tasks set in classrooms

Sub-category	Description
H1 Imaginative tasks	E.g. creative writing; compose a haiku on the theme: Spring
H2 Collecting evidence, problem-solving, deducing, reasoning tasks	E.g. discover by experiment which substance melts soonest; what law or principle can you deduce from a number of similar maths problems?
H3 Application tasks	Take some given knowledge and use it in a new situation: e.g. use French 'food' vocabulary to construct a menu
H4 Analysis tasks	Basically ask why? questions like – why does it work this way?
H5 Synthesis tasks	Synthesis involves taking things learned in one situation and using them in quite a different one, e.g. using knowledge of block graphs in maths to illustrate something in history
H6 Evaluation tasks	'Write a review of this book'

Improving the cognitive levels of tasks

If one casts one's mind back to the days before the National Curriculum, some educationists argued that much that passed for teaching was, in reality, management of the classroom environment. The key concern of many teachers was to sustain a high degree of student co-operation. In this situation, busy-ness became an end in itself: that students were occupied was more important than what they were occupied with.

One might have expected that the advent of the National Curriculum would change all that. Now, teachers would be frenetically trying to cover the syllabus and thus anxious that everything in class had a purpose. Tasks might be content-led, and perhaps data-laden rather than creative; but they would be purposeful.

In fact, like most generalisations, neither picture is totally true. There were intellectually demanding tasks before the National Curriculum, and after it. But both before and after it, too many tasks continue to be undemanding. Even during a period which I spent in the Further Education sector I was disappointed at the predictable and uninteresting, let alone undemanding, nature of much of the work. Copying from the board afflicted the lives even of 18 year-olds whose prime skill was not academic.

In the same way, when we studied the tasks set to accelerated examination sets working towards GCSE we found that, rather than becoming more intellectually demanding, tasks became increasingly banal. They were repetitive, involving much copying of notes and revision. They contributed little to a love of the subject studied, and nothing significant to a real understanding of it.

By contrast, tasks set to primary students tended to be consistently more demanding than those set in Key Stage 3. Why? Basically because, even in the post-National Curriculum era, many primary teachers devise work in a problem-solving format rather than allowing themselves to be totally content-dominated. This is a theme to which we shall return later.

So the key to task demand is in the nature of the tasks set: those characterised by Bloom's higher order thinking. Because this is so important, perhaps it will be beneficial at this point for you to practise recognising types of task. This, in turn, will help you to develop a mind-set in which you never compose a task for students without being conscious of what kind of a task it is. To this end you should now attempt Activity 9.

Activity 9
Practising task analysis
In Table 3 you will find 20 descriptions of real tasks which have been set to students in the early stages of Key Stage 3.
Use the task descriptions in Tables 1 and 2 to try to ascribe a sub-category (e.g. H1, L10, H3 etc.) to each of the 20 tasks.

Some of the tasks may seem very clear-cut. Others will be more ambiguous – perhaps due to the small amount of information which you have about them. Enter into the debate with yourself and try to come to a decision.

When you have carried out the exercise you will find a commentary and set of suggested answers on page 57.

Table 3

Twenty task descriptions for analysis

Tasks Sheet

1. 'In front of you is a set of tubes, stands and vessels, and a small quantity of the chemical. You've just watched me carry out the experiment, now each of you set up your own apparatus and carry it out in your own time.' (**Science**) ☐

2. 'Before we start using this folder let's make it look neat. Go through each blank page and draw a margin on it.' (**Humanities**) ☐

3. 'Here is your written assignment for homework; what makes The Diary of Adrian Mole Aged 13¾ so compelling a book for such a wide range of readers?' (**English**) ☐

4. 'Right, in the small groups you've chosen, go into separate corners and prepare your play for showing fear.' (**Drama**) ☐

5. 'We did this last week, so for homework it's page 33, examples 1–15.' (**Maths**) ☐

6. 'Here on the work-sheet is the story I have just told you about life in Sri Lanka; but there are some words missing. Your job is to fill in the blanks.' (**Geography**) ☐

7. 'Imagine you are Hadrian. Where else could you have put the wall and why?' (**History**) ☐

8. 'I have shown you how to find the area of this shape. Now work out how you could find the area of this one.' (**Maths**) ☐

9. 'Here's the obstacle course. You have to go round in the shortest possible time. The route you choose is important. Think about it for a minute – then when I say 'go', each person in turn . . . go!' (**PE**) ☐

10. 'Write 10 good reasons why Britain is likely to become a nation of geriatrics if the present trends continue.' (**Social Studies**)

11. 'Copy these notes from the board.' (**RE**)

12. 'When you've finished your story, illustrate it in any way you think appropriate.' (**English**)

13. 'Each group take a map. Follow the trail marked on your group's map. If you get it right you will find a yellow card at each point marked X on the map. Collect 4 yellow cards and come back here in the shortest possible time.' (**Geography, outdoors**)

14. 'First hand up: what has   (1) eyes as round as saucers
                      (2) a head that can point backwards
                      (3) one ear higher than the other?'
                      (**Environmental Studies**)

15. 'In this video recording about the causes of unemployment, compare the strength of the argument put forward by the two politicians.' (**General Studies**)

16. (Round the class)   '6 x 2?'
                          '5 x 4?'
                          '3 x 3?' (**Maths**)

17. 'We are going to devise attractive back-drops for a disco. Think of the Chromatography you did in science. Now apply that principle to devise patterns that could be rainbows of colour but using a wider range of colours than in the rainbow.' (**Art**)

18. 'Devise a questionnaire to discover which of the television programmes are most commonly watched by pupils in this school, and what your fellow pupils' viewing habits are.' (**Social Studies**)

19. 'Look at page 15. Summarise in your own words the main causes of the French Revolution listed there.' (**History**)

20. 'Here is a poster showing a typical Palestinian house in about 5 AD. Using the card, scissors and glue supplied, make your own model of a house like this.' (**RE**)

Raising the cognitive stakes in classrooms is an important part of the teacher's role, and should feature highly in the learning objectives for lessons. In this chapter we have looked at the contribution which task-setting can make to this process. In a further piece of research, undertaken in primary schools, I set out to look at the elements which could be incorporated into tasks (in this case, specifically tasks set in science lessons, though the principles apply across the curriculum) in order to ensure that students were being intellectually challenged. Table 4 identifies some of these elements.

Table 4

Cognitive components in classroom tasks: some active elements

Students can engage in . . .

- *Affective activity – learning from one another*
- *Acquiring new mechanical skills*
- *Acquiring new information by their own efforts*
- *Experiencing a phenomenon or event*
- *Working from diagrams, plans, instructions*
- *Recording their own findings*
- *Memorising new technical data*
- *Identifying e.g. specimens*
- *Estimating*
- *Guessing or hypothesising*
- *Analysing reasons or causes*
- *Testing hypotheses or concepts*
- *Formulating laws or generalisations*
- *Using evidence and drawing conclusions*
- *Solving problems*
- *Inventing new problems*
- *Evaluating situations and solutions*
- *Reporting orally and in writing*

Commentary on Activity 9

Task 1   If this task is simply copying the teacher's lead then it is low order, L9. In some circumstances it could be made to have elements of H3, but nothing in the description confirms this

Task 2   Low order L3: this contributes nothing to learning as such, unless it is a deliberate attempt to improve the manual skills of small children

Task 3   An evaluative task – so H6

Task 4   This requires some imagination in conveying an emotion, and is higher order – H1

Task 5   Revision, L8

Task 6   The key is the words 'have just told you' – so this is reinforcement, L11

Task 7   A superb task involving elements of several higher order skills – H4 and H6 are strongest

Task 8   One assumes that the two shapes are similar so the task is Application – H3

Task 9   The shortest route has to be analysed, so H4

Task 10   The key word is 'why' – so H4

Task 11   L4 – there is no cognitive demand in this

Task 12   This could have overtones of H1, imagination; more often it is merely L3 – a device for keeping students of different abilities together

Task 13   This is an application task, H3, because the students must apply their orienteering skill to find the cards. Some teachers want to score this low because it does not require conventional classroom-based work: this is an error

Task 14 Problem-solving, using evidence and hypothesising: H2, elements of H6

Task 15 Evaluation, H6

Task 16 Almost certainly rote learning – L 8, L1 1

Task 17 Transfer of scientific knowledge to the field of Art – i.e. synthesis, H5

Task 18 Strongly H2, though with overtones of other higher order skills

Task 19 'Summarise' suggests that this is a task which involves given/existing data, not the manipulation of data. This makes it low order, possibly L8

Task 20 The equipment is provided and the task seems uncomplicated copying as it is described: so L3. It could be made higher order if there are elements of technology incorporated into the task, but there is no evidence of this.

Chapter 5

Factors in effective task-setting

In the previous chapter we established that classroom tasks are things which teachers ask students to do, that they can be very varied in nature, and that they make varying intellectual or cognitive demands. In this chapter it is the intention to look at the skills the teacher needs in order to set effective tasks.

To this end, we can begin by looking at a list of pre-requisites which help towards effective task setting.

Table 5

Pre-requisites for task effectiveness

An effective classroom task . . .

■ *has a clear purpose in the mind of the teacher;*
■ *has a purpose which is communicated to the student;*
■ *is couched in a form/language which is suitable for the target student group;*

- *is interesting;*
- *is of a cognitive level such as will stimulate and stretch the target students;*
- *is one of a series which will vary in form and demand;*
- *meets the needs of the target students;*
- *has clearly explained parameters.*

Each of the items in Table 5 is worthy of some discussion.

The task has a clear purpose in the mind of the teacher

This item need not detain us for long, since Chapters 1–3 of this book have laid down the processes for establishing the learning objectives for whatever it is that the teacher wishes to achieve. Just as lessons and longer-term sections of curriculum need to be formulated alongside clear learning objectives, so each individual task within the scheme of work needs to be equally well planned.

The task has a purpose which is communicated to the student

But however well the teacher plans, that planning is only half effective if it remains in the mind of the teacher alone. To share learning objectives with students – and that includes the purposes for individual tasks – is to take a long stride in the direction of achievement of those purposes. Really good tasks are those in which the student begins with a clear sense of purpose. It is just like setting out on a journey: being lost on the back roads is fascinating on occasion, but most journeys have a purpose which cannot be achieved unless one arrives at the destination.

The task is couched in a form/language which is suitable for the target student group

In the same way, only tasks which are comprehensible are really likely to succeed. Effective tasks are couched in words which the students – all the students in the class – will understand; and the processes of carrying out the task must be clear. This means that tasks have to be explained clearly and good instructions given. At this point in the book the assumption is that a common task is being set to all students simultaneously. This is the commonest kind of task-setting, but later it will be necessary to deal with the implications of differentiation and dealing with ranges of ability within the task.

The task is interesting

This item should be self-evident. There is a growing body of opinion which suggests that students have a right to expect that teachers will make school work interesting: in some cases of high truancy, for example, it has been suggested that the key factor is a failure of interest caused by boring teaching. As professionals we have to take this view seriously: and it manifests itself, too, in the view that – since students have access to a range of media outside school, much of which is engaging to them – their in-school experience has to compete to survive. Even if neither of these arguments is, of itself, sufficiently persuasive to you, your own professionalism should require you to take the item seriously.

The task is of a cognitive level such as will stimulate and stretch the target students

Chapter 4 dealt with the details of cognitive level. Here the message is that tasks which make few demands rapidly bore students. Most students like a degree of challenge – even the least able like to feel that they are not simply time-wasting, or time-filling. The greater the degree of realism in the task, the more likely it is to capture the students' imaginations.

The task is one of a series which will vary in form and demand

For the same reason, over time, the tasks set by teachers need to vary in scope and style. Teachers, like others, tend to drop into grooves. X works well, so X becomes the staple diet of the classroom, and soon everyone is bored by X – first the students, but ultimately the teacher, too. Variety is, in that sense, the spice of life. Just as the serial story or the episodic soap opera presents a new and critical situation at each interval, so lessons have to have that flavour of freshness. This is demanding of the teacher, and needs attention to longer-term planning to bring it about.

The task meets the needs of the target students

Again, this sounds simplistic; but the fact is that research tends to suggest that only about half of all classroom tasks set are actually 'matched' to the level of need of the students. Thus too many tasks are either too hard or, usually, too easy for the target group. Differentiation, which is dealt with later, can help to solve this problem: but careful planning in the first instance, along with properly formulated learning objectives, may be a preventative step.

The task has clearly explained parameters

Finally in this short review of pre-requisites we need to draw attention to the teacher's willingness to draw boundaries round the task. This will include such instructions as the length of time to take on it, the number of words to write, or the constraints to be put in place. For example, if the task were to compose a short play the teacher might limit it to four minutes' duration, on a prescribed topic, with three characters only. This item also includes indications to the students about the criteria upon which the task is going to be assessed. Such criteria should be stated 'up front', so that students are aware when working of what things require priority attention.

This short review of the pre-requisites of task-setting has set the scene for you to have a look at your own practice using Activity 10.

Activity 10
Reviewing your own task-setting

Look back over the tasks which you have set for a term.
Use the items in Table 5 to assess how effectively you prepare for your own task-setting for students.
What items do you satisfy consistently?
What do you need to review about your own practice?

When you have completed Activity 10, look at the task example set out in Figure 8, page 42. This example (from a pre-GCSE class) picks up the final point above – about setting pre-agreed criteria, which then effectively become the assessment grid against which student performance on the task is judged.

Taking stock of the task-setting process

So far, in the previous chapter and this one, the aim has been two-fold:

- to examine the nature of classroom tasks
- to get you thinking about the skills you need to make your own task-setting successful.

At this juncture it is appropriate to deal with two other topics which are extremely significant in the task-setting process. These relate to the period before a task is set, and to the period after a task is completed by the class.

The learner's prior knowledge

Earlier in the chapter we looked at some of the pre-requisites that make task-setting effective. One important factor was omitted there in order to give it individual attention: the learner's prior knowledge.

The basic thesis here goes like this. In order for a task to be effective it has to match the learner's current knowledge, understanding and skills; it has to meet the student's need and thus move him/her on on one or more of these fronts. Matching and meeting thus become twin principles for task-setting. However well formulated the task, and however interesting it might potentially be, it cannot succeed unless it matches and meets the student's current situation.

In practice, however, almost all task-setting is done without any systematic attention to this issue. Imagine two extreme but common scenarios:

- It is your first day with a new primary class, the first day of the Autumn Term. You may know the students' names, you may even have seen them carry out tasks (such as presenting an assembly) from time to time. But on what basis do you set the first tasks in those first few hours with the class?

■ You are a teacher in Year 7 of a secondary school, and today you meet the children in your class for the first time. They have been drawn from eight different primary schools. You want to get on with the learning process and set them some homework; but how do you know what they have in common or of what any individual is capable?

Common enough experiences; and there are worse. For example, think of the plight of the supply teacher who meets a new class on every assignment!

What is needed is a strategy: a means for finding out what students know, understand and can do. Is it possible that research can help us here?

Certainly the literature of task-setting has some answers, so these need some scrutiny for what they might offer the teacher.

1. Diagnostic interview

This is a process whereby the teacher discusses aspects of the current learning at some length with each individual student in order to try to piece together the student's operational thinking and the understandings on which these are based. This is a useful method. The major drawback is time: in a normal classroom it would not be possible for a teacher to give each student enough attention to achieve this very often. However, properly applied, the technique is a good one. It can be used once or twice a year – for example, to establish students' prior knowledge at the beginning of a year, and progress and development at the half-way stage. It can be used with students with learning difficulties, especially where student:teacher ratios are favourable. It can be used with an individual student who has a learning problem with respect to a specific piece of work. The system of tutorial interviews, which is increasingly finding favour in the secondary sector, is built on this principle.

2. Word association and sorting tasks

This is rather a specialised approach, but consists of presenting the student with a word to which he or she responds with the first word they think of. By repeating this process a trained operator (such as a psychologist) can establish whether a student is making connections between linked concepts. The method may have some clinical value, but is impractical for the classroom teacher.

3. Writing a definition

Another approach is to ask the students to write (or select from alternative) definitions which relate to the subject matter being taught. The teacher can judge from the definitions written (or the choices made) the level of sophistication of the students' understandings. This is useful in some circumstances and subjects (more so in science than in a foreign language perhaps), and has the advantage that it is a fairly economic process in terms of lesson time involved.

4. Testing

This is a very crude method for assessing prior learning. Most tests assess knowledge: but many educationists would argue that students become expert at simply listening to teachers and regurgitating acceptable answers. This process may lead to acceptable or better test scores, but it has little to tell us about the students' understandings. It is predicated on a view of knowledge as content and is inadequate as a professional activity.

5. Consulting records

One way with which to begin an assessment of students' prior knowledge is to read the records sent on from one class teacher to another, or from one school to another. There is a lot of research which suggests that this is rarely done! If the research is accurate, and it probably is, then one has to ask why records of this kind are compiled anyway. Clearly the answer is in terms of fulfilling the baser requirements of accountability rather than in terms of the furthering of any educational aims. But even where records are carefully compiled, are insightful, and aimed at usefulness, they are often ignored.

It is common enough to hear the excuse that the teacher or school wants to assess the child for themselves and without prejudice.

Phrases like: 'fresh start' or 'clean sheet' abound. This attitude has a kind of spurious persuasiveness drawn from the rules of fair play about it – but it isn't really very professional. To read records does not mean that one has to be biased by them – objectivity is part of professionalism just as is avoiding prejudice. So records have some part to play in the process of informing teachers about students.

6. Feedback

In a previous book in this series it was suggested that teachers often use classroom questions to gauge students' knowledge, and so these questions form a kind of assessment of prior knowledge and current understanding. The value of this is not in doubt, subject to one important proviso: that the questions probe not just regurgitated content, but explore the students' mind-sets and the structure of their understanding and thinking. This brings the process closer to the diagnostic interview described above in point 1, but in a whole-class or group context rather than one-to-one.

Bowring-Carr and West-Burnham point to an important implication in the approach which has been described here. They note that assessing prior knowledge is to begin from where the student is. This is no new concept: the Plowden Report (1967) said exactly that. But Bowring-Carr and West-Burnham emphasise:

> . . .the culture of the school will have to change; it will need to change from one in which implicitly and explicitly the main emphasis is on enabling teachers to teach, to one in which the main emphasis is on enabling children to learn.
>
> *(Bowring-Carr C. and West-Burham J. (1997)* **Effective Learning in Schools,** *London: Pitman, p106)*

Some may feel that this view contradicts the fundamental basis on which a book on teaching skills is based: teaching skills are for teachers not learners! But I would challenge that view. Even Bowring-Carr and West-Burnham need teachers – though teachers re-defined as the managers of learning. Such managers need 'teaching' skills: the facilitative skills which impart understanding to others. That is precisely what this book, and this series, is about.

So, from this chapter and the last, we have established that effective task-setting requires:

- the formulation of sound learning objectives;
- the systematic assessment of the learner's prior knowledge;
- the fulfilment of the pre-requisites for 'effective tasks' described above on pages 59–62;
- the building in to tasks of appropriate cognitive demand;
- the establishment of pre-agreed criteria to indicate to students what will constitute success in tackling the task.

These steps lead us inevitably to look at the recording of student achievement once one or more tasks have been completed and assessed. Before tackling this next chapter, however, it may be valuable to take stock of your own approaches to assessing students' prior learning by undertaking Activity 11.

Activity 11
Assessing students' prior knowledge

In a paragraph or two, write a critical analysis of how you assess the prior learning of your students. Make sure that you answer the following questions in your analysis:

- What use do you make of
  - records from other teachers
  - testing
  - diagnostic techniques
  - other methods?
- How effective are the processes you use?
- How do you use the information you discover?
- What could you do to improve your techniques?

Now draw up an action plan for assessing the prior knowledge of students you encounter for the first time, e.g. at the beginning of the Autumn Term or on starting a new job.

Chapter 6

Tracking and recording students' progress

Recording achievement: the key questions

With the task-setting process firmly established, attention shifts to the recording of the outcomes from the tasks. The following are the key questions which every teacher has to answer about recording students' achievements.

- Why record?
- How should the recording occur?
- What should be recorded?
- For what audiences are the records intended?
- Where are records kept?
- How often are they up-dated?

The following paragraphs take a first look at each of these questions;

though it should be emphasised that schools and individual teachers need to answer the questions within their own contexts.

Why record?

The fundamental reason for recording is so that the progress of each student can be tracked. There are other reasons, too:

- so that teachers can assess whether learning objectives are being met;
- so that there is feedback to the teacher about the effectiveness of lessons e.g. whether content is explained clearly and is understood;
- to inform future planning.

Ofsted inspectors are specially primed to look at this last point. They try to assess, in every lesson, whether feedback to the teacher is being used to inform what is happening in the short-term and to influence future lesson intentions. Other implicit reasons for gathering assessment data are covered in the sub-sections which follow.

For the moment we need to pause over the factors which have given assessment and recording a poor press with teachers over recent years. These have been related to the controversies which have been generated about a) whether students are making better or worse progress now than in previous generations, and b) whether crude test results can be used as data against which the effectiveness of schools can be measured. In a book of this nature it is, perhaps, important to take a stance over each of these issues.

On the first, it is almost impossible for anyone, however well or badly motivated, to make a judgement. In times gone by many students left school very early, or hardly attended. There is plenty of evidence of gross illiteracy and poor mathematical performance among youngsters and adults from the first and second world wars, for example. In our present environment some educationists would argue that the average school student has to learn much more in quantity, and a far wider range of knowledge, information and skills; so the fact that some fail to do so effectively is inevitable. Let us be clear: there is no room for complacency here. But a fifteen year-old of today is unlikely to be less 'educated' than a fifteen year-old of times past. That does not mean that the eleven years of statutory education have been well spent or successful; it simply means that comparisons are meaningless: the student of 1890 may have written in a fine copper-plate but didn't have to master the Internet. The root question is: are we doing all we can, as well as we can, to equip all our citizens for life in the 21st century?

On the second issue, that of published results, for example SATs and GCSE results, there are quite blatant crudities in this system that are so obvious and so crass that even politicians should not be persuaded by them. Clearly, schools do not all start at the same point: facilities and buildings vary, the socio-economic climates of communities differ, the expectations of parents vary from one place to another and so on. To pretend that these factors are not significant is unintelligent. To suggest that it is only a matter of trying harder that will equalise the performance of all schools and of all students is ludicrous beyond belief. But there should be measures of how well schools and students are improving. To demand and monitor these is reasonable; to use them as objective measures of success and failure without contextual information is banal.

For the teacher in the classroom, recording is a tool of the trade providing a source of feedback both to the teacher and, critically, to the student.

How should the recording occur?

Teachers need written, objective records to which they can refer. But this does not mean that a single standardised system of recording can be adopted to meet every contingency. Back in the old days, when I began my teaching career, schools were equally concerned with recording: but the records consisted of a string of marks out of 10 or out of 20 for items not clearly identified, with occasional percentages for end-of-term examinations. This system was neat, provided plenty of comparative statistical data, and kept everyone happy; though it was largely meaningless!

Records of performance can take many forms, and the simplest way of illustrating this is simply to list some and to let you, from your experience, add to the lists:

- Short accounts of diagnostic conversations with the student.
- Marks for periodic revision tests.
- Scores and/or comments against performance criteria for specific tasks.
- Mock SAT scores or exam results.
- Progress on National Curriculum Attainment Targets.
- Examples of specially interesting work or work which illustrates a student's difficulties (e.g. a page of work with b,d,p written backwards).
- Student self-assessments (about which more will be said later).
- Analyses of the student's cognitive achievements on specific tasks.
- Teacher summaries about students' knowledge, understanding and skill levels.
- Notes, e.g. about a student's particularly interesting oral contribution to a lesson.

You will note that the emphasis in this list is not about scores, it is about teacher analysis of student performance: an important distinction.

What should be recorded?

The answer to this question is implicit in the previous sub-section: anything and everything that is relevant to understanding the ability and performance of each individual student.

For what audiences are the records intended?

The prime audience for records which track student progress is the . . . student. This is certainly a very different answer from the traditional one . . . the teacher. Both, of course, are important: but if the teacher is the facilitator of learning, then it is the learner who is at the heart of the recording process.

But, there are other audiences too. In an age of accountability, the teacher needs records in order to satisfy a number of people with legitimate reasons for knowing what the records reveal: the parents, the headteacher, other members of the department in a secondary school, colleagues in a primary school, teachers to whom students are handed on (on moving home or school), inspectors. The form of the recording may vary slightly from audience to audience; but this will be partly for the school to adopt a policy about.

Where are records kept?

The first answer is: securely. Records are confidential and should not be left on view. They need to be locked up or, if on data-base, then concealed with a code. Written records should not be thrown into skips or waste-bins, but shredded; and certainly never left revealed on the car seat in the staff car park! Again, there should be school policies on these issues.

How often are they up-dated?

While records are distinguished by quality not quantity, there should be enough recording by individual teachers to ensure good knowledge of each student. Schools, including departments or year groups, will have rules and policies about what is an acceptable minimum.

To summarise, we might cast an eye over what government documents say about the value of assessment and the recording of progress and achievement. The collected wisdom seems to be:

ASSESSMENT AND RECORDING
- are at the heart of the learning process;
- support continuity between teachers, classes, schools;
- identify progress made by students;
- feed back to strengthen curriculum and teaching;
- help in future planning;
- improve student learning through feedback;
- should be part of the teaching/learning cycle.

This is a good moment at which to review your own practice in recording by carrying out the task in Activity 12.

Activity 12
Reviewing your recording systems

Revisit the issues discussed above, and try to evaluate the extent to which your recording practices are effective.

- Why do you record? Have you a clearly articulated policy? Has the school a policy? Are you fulfilling it?

- How does the recording occur? How systematic are you about your recording?

- What do you record? Is the range sufficiently varied? Does it take account of the students' perceptions of their progress?

- For what audiences are your records intended? Have you systems that allow you to meet the demands of each audience?

- Where are your records kept? Is confidentiality ensured?

- How often are your records up-dated?

Try to find an opportunity to share your ideas with one or more colleagues, and see what you can learn from their practice.

Recording achievement: some additional issues

The previous section of this chapter established the basic guidelines for recording students' progress. But a number of other matters are worth some discussion before leaving this subject.

1. Marking work

Good marking practice demands that the teacher brings to the process some sympathetic skills. Most marking will probably take place away from the classroom, but sometimes it is useful to mark alongside the student so that the student can gain an insight into the process and can have the immediacy of being able to see and contribute to the marking process. Marking should always be done within a reasonable time: it is useful to have a consistent rule about this such as 'Homework handed in each Monday, work returned each following Monday'. Nothing frustrates students more than work which is turned around slowly. Work must always be marked: failure to mark is culpable and a denial of professionalism. Set less work and mark it effectively rather than more work and skimp the process, might be a good rule.

Commenting should always contain a reference to strengths as well as weaknesses – and guidelines for future improvement. Personally, given a choice, I prefer to write comments at the end or on a separate sheet rather than deface the student's work. In the primary school in which I work we have a system of comment sheets for major pieces of work such as the termly project (see Table 6). This is exactly the same pattern as is used for my MBA students in the university (Table 7). Comment sheets should be based on the criteria agreed for each piece of work (see below).

2. Pre-agreed criteria

On page 42 (Figure 8) the issue of pre-agreed criteria was discussed and illustrated. In recording student outcomes it is important to keep the marks/grades and comments for all the criteria, and not reduce the process to a global score which indicates little or nothing.

3. Self-assessment

From time to time it is quite reasonable to ask students to assess their own work. This may happen in a variety of circumstances or operate in several different ways. For example, a very able student may be asked to critique his/her own work: an exercise which stops the more able from skimping on quality. Or a whole class may use the answer-book to check their own maths exercise. This is a mechanical task which can save the teacher time – though the outcome still needs a professional eye to see what mistakes are being made and by whom!

Self-assessment helps to make students more responsible for their own learning; and is thus more appropriate for a 21st century approach to learning.

Table 6

A sample of a comment sheet for a primary school project

Topic:	*The Tudors*
Main focus:	*History. Focus of assessment: Elizabethan writing*
Key issue:	*Empathy (characters, events, feelings, understanding)*

English:	1 *Speaking and listening*
	2 *Reading*
	3 *Writing*
	■ *spelling*
	■ *handwriting*
	■ *presentation*
	■ *overall success (purpose, audience, style)*
Landmark assessments:	1 *Story of a holiday adventure*
	a) *Punctuation, including dialogue conventions*
	b) *Overall success of the writing (in terms of purpose, audience, style)*
	2 *Story of exploration*
	a) *Punctuation*
	b) *Overall success*

Table 7

An example of a comment sheet for a university MBA assignment

Student:	_____ Date: _____
Title:	_____
	_____

Introduction (title, scope, relevance, contents pages, outline research questions, order and rationale)

_____ /10 _____

Literature (appropriateness, range, relevance, analytical treatment)

_____ /15 _____

Investigation (appropriateness of methods, justification, execution)

_____ /15 _____

Analysis (methods used, use made of data and appropriate manipulation, maximising outcomes)

_____ /25 _____

Conclusion (effectiveness of 'drawing out the messages' and applying them to real situations)

_____ /10 _____

Presentation (clarity of argument, layout)

_____ /10 _____

Overall

_____ /15 _____

TOTAL   %   GRADE   _____

4. Peer assessment

This needs careful handling, but should not be written off as a technique. One of the important lessons in life is that one's work and performance is judged by others; so it is vital to learn to handle that early in life. For example, in primary schools children sometimes swap books to mark work – rather like self-assessment except it is between partners. On a more sophisticated level, the teacher might ask students in a secondary design class to design a model according to pre-agreed criteria and put the results up for scrutiny by the class. Some students will find this a painful process, and considerable skill is required of the teacher to protect the vulnerable.

5. Meta-cognition

This is a large topic, and has been dealt with earlier in the book.

6. Learning contracts

The use of learning contracts can be helpful in some circumstances. Reluctant learners may benefit from the security of knowing exactly what they have to do and when, and how the teacher will respond. I use a form of learning contract with less able youngsters in primary school. They are withdrawn from lessons for a period each week for additional help, but have to reinforce this time by undertaking some extra work at home. This extra work is assessed in the next withdrawal period. Some students find this a difficult discipline; but failure to conform to the requirement impedes the next withdrawal period and therefore their overall progress. In some cases I have had to form the contract with both the student and with a parent who agrees to oversee the work at home. The result is often increased interest from the home and improved performance by the student. If the work is effectively carried out there is often a small incentive in the form of a 'game' of some kind during the next session – though few of the students realise the 'games' are actually learning exercises in disguise!

7. Periodic tutorial review

In passing, it was mentioned earlier that some schools are now assigning students to tutors who sit down quietly with individuals and review progress from time to time. In a few schools, older students fulfil this role for younger pupils in place of teachers, and it seems to work effectively. Tutorial review means that someone is overseeing progress, and that adds an incentive to make some! In the context of review by a teacher, recording can be useful.

8. Reflective teaching

Finally in this review of issues in relation to recording, it is appropriate to mention the philosophy of reflective teaching. Reflective teachers scrutinise their own performance, including the lessons they learn through the tasks they set and how the students respond to these. Sometimes they do this using a written log of some kind; but even carrying out the Activities in this book of skills is a way of reflecting on your own teaching. Reflective teachers are those who thus continuously review and up-date their skills, using practice and outcomes as the basis for moving their own professionalism on.

Conclusion

At the start of this chapter we had established that the following criteria are essential to effective task-setting:

- the formulation of sound learning objectives;
- the systematic assessment of the learner's prior knowledge;
- the fulfilment of the pre-requisites for 'effective tasks' described above on pages 59–62;
- the building in to tasks of appropriate cognitive demand as described in Chapter 4;
- the establishment of pre-agreed criteria to indicate to students what will constitute success in tackling the task.

To these this chapter has added:

- the importance of marking work using a variety of techniques;

- the need to track student progress systematically through task responses;

- the need to communicate with students and others the outcomes of progress review;

- the need to think out ways of involving students in taking responsibility for their own progress;

- the need to develop one's self professionally through a reflexive approach.

In the next chapter we move to look at task setting in practice, and some example of tasks for analysis.

Chapter 7

Task-setting in practice

Introduction

In the previous three chapters we have looked at the nature of classroom tasks and their cognitive demands, at the skills of setting effective tasks, and at assessing and recording progress through task-setting. In this chapter we look at an example of task-setting in action to try to work over the practical issues and problems. The task described is a real task which was actually used: and it could be set to any class in Key Stages 2 or 3 with minor adaptations of context and content, for example by adapting to a different lesson length or by changing the subject matter.

The task

Our teacher – we will call her Miss Smith – teaches in a small primary school. The students are divided into Key Stage 1 and Key Stage 2 classes, and Miss Smith teaches Key Stage 2. She has pupils in Years 3 to 6 in the same class, and the class is about average in size at 34 students. The classroom is just large enough for this class size: the students sit in fours, grouped round tables, with the exception of two students who are at a small table in a rather cramped corner. There is the advantage of a small work-space through folding doors which lead off the classroom, but this has to be used with care as students can disappear out of the teacher's eye-line.

The students have been studying Ancient Greece as part of the National Curriculum. Though the main thrust of the work has been historical and geographical, this theme has governed their work in English, RE, story-time and science as well. They have had a visit from a music specialist talking about ancient instruments, and from an architect who has explained some of the principles behind Greek buildings using specially-made build-it-yourself kits which the children could put together. The term and the theme are drawing to a close, and the teacher wants to draw together some of the threads of the work.

Miss Smith is also aware of some of the social factors which affect this class. Teaching across ages is not easy: and one constant need is to provide activities in which everyone can play a part and which cater for each student's level of maturity. There is also the intellectual issue: a four-year age-span also represents a myriad of variations in intellectual ability *combined* with emotional maturity.

Miss Smith decides to dedicate the equivalent of a school day to the 'finale' of the Greek theme. But she feels that a whole day may be too long for some students: so she decides to use three of the four sessions on Day 1 (having begun the day, as is usual in this school, with some spelling and number work), plus a final session on Day 2.

This is the context. Now she has to decide on the task.

Miss Smith decides that the students should write a newspaper. One purpose of this task is that it draws together the work which has been done over the term. Another is that it contributes to the English curriculum by helping the students to identify audiences and to write in appropriate styles. The third consideration is that everyone, from Year 3 to Year 6 can contribute. Finally, she has a further learning purpose. For some time she has been concerned that the students do not work quickly enough, and with sufficient focus, unless she oversees them. She is concerned to develop greater self-motivation, and she thinks that the newspaper task can deliver this. This, then, is the basic plan.

Miss Smith decides that, of the four sessions available, she must spend a part of the first session sharing with the students what they have to do, and explaining the purposes of the task. She also needs some discussion time about the nature of newspapers, so that the students share the concept with her and each other. Her basic time-plan looks like this:

DAY 1

Session 1:   Explain the task

Talk about the nature of newspapers

Get everyone started

Sessions 2&3:   Everyone working on a specific aspect of the newspaper

DAY 2

Session 4:   The newspaper comes together.

Getting started

So Miss Smith is now ready for Session 1. She begins with an introductory talk lasting a few minutes in which she brings to the students' notice a local paper with a powerful headline. The children talk about the headline; and then Miss Smith goes on to ask about what else we could expect to find in newspapers. She elicits the kinds of answers she hopes for (features, advertisements, sports pages, pictures). They talk about who reads the paper, what makes it interesting, the style in which different parts are written, the kinds of pictures that are used and for what purposes.

She then goes on to ask what kind of newspaper might have been produced in Ancient Greece if the technology had been available: there were plenty of good observers and writers, so what would have the papers reported?

Finally, she moves on to newspaper production. Who writes? How are the pictures produced? Who puts the paper together? and so on.

The students are quite enthusiastic about all this; and excited when she says that they are going to produce their own paper.

It is thus a joint decision that the class feels it should write the paper for their parents – to display in the waiting area the next day for parents to read as they come to collect their youngsters from school. It is a joint decision, too, that not everyone can do the same job, so tasks have to be allocated. Miss Smith is appointed the Proprietor; and she has to appoint editors, reporters and so on.

A key issue to be stressed by Miss Smith is the time factor. Deadlines are explained. Now everyone is ready, and keyed up, to start work. All that remains is for jobs to be allocated.

Three older students are appointed editors: two for text and one for pictures. They have two roles: to choose the material to be included, and to fit it into the space available. (This is a manual process, since not enough computers are available to word process the whole product: though some parts of it – such as the title page will be produced using computers and duplicating facilities.)

A number of students are allocated to the advertising department; others to picture production; some to writing features; some as reporters. A couple are appointed cartoonists. Others become sports specialists. Deadlines are re-inforced. The work begins.

After lunch, in Sessions 3 and 4, the work continues apace. The teacher is able to spend a lot of time monitoring individuals and their contributions, discussing content and style. The editorial staff have set up an office in the work-space next door. They have put a notice on the door which reads: 'Editors' Office – knock to enter'. They are preparing the large sheets of paper on which they will make their layouts of the final designs for the paper and are working on producing the computer-generated title page.

The feature writers are having to think about what kinds of features, and what subject matter, they want to cover. The cartoonists are mocking up cartoon layouts and deciding on subject matter. The sports reporters are thinking up what they can say about Ancient Greek sporting events. The news journalists are trawling what they know about Ancient Greece to find good copy for the front pages. Advertisers have to imagine what Ancient Greeks would find attractive to buy . . . and so on.

As the afternoon goes on, things take shape and some products are beginning to emerge. The Proprietor has to remind the work-force about deadlines; and the editors have rejected some early copy because it isn't good enough! Commitment is high and the line between fantasy and reality is becoming blurred.

At the end of the day, the whole newspaper team comes together to take stock. The editors say what they still need. The Proprietor urges deadlines. Some pages are taking shape and can be shown and shared, but there is still a long way to go and only one session tomorrow in which to make the deadline. Everyone goes home with a few butterflies in the stomach – not least Miss Smith.

The next day is a fine one: that's good because poor weather makes the students fractious and today they have to be very focused. The pressure is building. The two text editors have their work cut out now receiving, judging, amending, spacing the contributions. The picture editor wants better material. The duplicator is playing up, but the headlines still need magnification on the copier. Everyone is struggling. As the session proceeds, the pages take shape. One or two students whose work has been rejected by the editors go away and produce something better because they don't want to be left out.

Just when she thinks she is winning, Miss Smith is approached by the text editors. They have a half-page blank and want her to contribute something within the next twenty minutes to fill the space! She has to sit at a word processor and write, against the clock. There are three minutes left to the end of the session: and the newspaper has to be published when the bell goes. They make it, but it's a close call! Spontaneous cheer.

Outcomes

Miss Smith has achieved her aim of getting a newspaper, and getting it by the deadline. Later she has time to take stock of precisely what the newspaper consists. What follows here is a selection only of the contributions.

From the news section of the Athens Recorder:

Could it have happened?

A school in Athens has been attacked. Several children have been killed, and two teachers including the headmaster Helos Ancos. The Greek police have sealed off the area completely. Some of the children have given a description, a clear description.

Here is the description given by six-year-old Dephos Elios: Dark hair, dark skin, dirty, tall, slim build and big feet.

If you see him ring Athens 02132596. (Y5)

Kidnapped!

Yesterday a girl aged nineteen was kidnapped in the market. School children like Theseus King, Jason Sarjent and Timothy Ricket saw this terrible thing happen. They have explained that a black, dark man called Hades invaded the market. Beware! He will take your children. Demeter, Kores' mother, has put a terrible spell on Greece till she gets her child back. . . . (Y4)

Gods

Yesterday Poseidon got angry and made an earthquake. Here are some witnesses' accounts of how it was.

Σαμ: It was terrible, you can't explain.

Ασλη: It was terrible.   (Y3)

The Answer

A scientist called Archimedes has invented a screw to lift water up from one level to another.

I spoke to a farmer called Philippos who has used the Archimedes screw and this is what he said:

"It was very good for watering the crops. It was quicker. It was very good and I will use the Archimedes screw every day."

                                                              (Y6)

The Trojan Horse

Today in Troy there was an accident and this is Elizabeth Richards reporting from Athens in Greece.

It all started when the clever Athenians made a wooden horse and filled it with soldiers. The next day the Athenians pushed the horse to the gates of Troy.

The Trojans thought it was a gift from the gods. So they pulled the horse into the city.

That night the soldiers crept out of the horse and destroyed the city. So that was the end of Troy.

                                                              (Y3)

From the theatre page:

Alexander the Great in Costume

Here at the best theatre in Greece you can watch one of the most important persons in Greece, Alexander the Great.

He is playing the part of a cruel, heartless king who would turn anyone away who came for help.

The character does not bring Alexander's true personality out, for Alexander is a kind helpful person, the opposite of the character he is playing. (Y4)

Oh no it isn't!

Oh yes it is! A brilliant performance put on by Athens' best theatre.

The play they put on was about Kore, snatched by the evil god of the underworld. It was a great success, with the famous female actor Euripidia Annalayas as Kore, and the famous male actor Sophocles Annalayas as Hades. It was brilliant.

A few lucky locals were acting as villagers.

I asked one of the theatre-goers who said: "It was excellent the way Kore screamed." (Y5)

Taking stock

The purpose of describing Miss Smith's task and its outcomes at some length has been to give you, the reader, some basis on which to begin to make judgements about classroom tasks using a task other than one which you have invented yourself.

The task described above could have been used in a variety of subject areas, especially (but not exclusively) in the humanities. It could also have been adapted for use by students of any age up to the end of Key Stage 3.

What is important about the task is the extent to which it reveals the strengths and weaknesses of the task-setting. For this reason you might like to start by analysing the task against some of the criteria which were discussed in Chapter 5. To do this you can attempt Activity 13.

Activity 13

Analysing the effectiveness of Miss Smith's task

Read over Chapter 7 again using the criteria listed there and below to try to assess how effective you think Miss Smith's task-setting was.

Item	Positive features	Negative features
1. The task had a clear purpose in the mind of the teacher.		
2. The purpose was communicated to the students.		
3. The task was couched in suitable language for the target group.		
4. The task was interesting.		
5. The task had a cognitive level to stretch and stimulate the students.		
6. The task was one of a series , varying in form and demand.		
7. The task met the needs of the students.		
8. The task had clearly explained parameters.		

Having established how effective this task was for its intended audience, you should think about issues relating to the cognitive demand of the task in a little more detail. Activity 14 will start you on this process.

Activity 14
The cognitive elements of Miss Smith's task

Look down the list below, which is taken from Table 4 (on page 56).

Use the items in the list to decide which cognitive elements were present (as far as you can judge from the evidence presented in this chapter) in Miss Smith's task.

Remember, evidence may be found either in the account of the task or from the ways in which the students interpreted it.

Component	Present (✓)	Not present (✗)
1. Affective activity		
2. Acquiring new mechanical skills		
3. Acquiring new information by students' own efforts		
4. Experiencing a phenomenon or event		
5. Working from diagrams, instructions etc.		
6. Recording students' own findings		
7. Memorising new data		
8. Identifying e.g. specimens		
9. Estimating		
10. Guessing or hypothesising		

11. Analysing reasons
    or causes
12. Testing hypotheses,
    concepts
13. Formulating laws
    or generalisations
14. Using evidence,
    drawing conclusions
15. Solving problems

When you have completed the grid, ask yourself which of the missing components could and should have been built into the task.

Finally, tackle Activity 15.

Activity 15

Deciding on the cognitive level of Miss Smith's task, and recording the students' performance

Re-read the section about cognitive levels of tasks on pages 49–54. Then decide whether you rate this task overall a higher order task or a low order one. Perhaps parts of it fall to each category – if so, which parts are higher order and which low order?

Now consider the issues about recording discussed in Chapter 6. We are not told how Miss Smith recorded the outcomes of her task. How would you have set about this?

Summary

In Chapters 4–7 an attempt has been made to look systematically at the factors which make teachers' task-setting effective, and at the demands which tasks make on students. A basic thesis of these chapters has been that task-setting is a skill which can worked upon and improved through a little focused thought and by incorporating an appropriate level of task demand for the student audience.

In the task example provided by Miss Smith (because she was teaching children of mixed ages and abilities) we were also moving towards a crucial topic which has not been dealt with explicitly so far in this book, but which is the subject of the next three chapters: differentiation.

Chapter 8

The purpose of differentiation

(MATERIAL FOR THIS CHAPTER AND THE NEXT HAS BEEN TAKEN IN PART FROM AN ARTICLE PREVIOUSLY PUBLISHED IN *EDUCATIONAL STUDIES* VOLUME 23 NUMBER 3, 1997. MY THANKS ARE DUE TO THE EDITOR OF EDUCATIONAL STUDIES, TO CARFAX PUBLISHING, AND TO THE CO-AUTHOR OF THE ARTICLE, CAROLLE KERRY, FOR PERMISSION TO USE THIS MATERIAL.)

Some traditional approaches

Differentiation is the process whereby the levels of tasks set to students in class or for homework are matched to the known levels of performance and potential of the individual students involved.

These levels relate to issues we have discussed earlier in this book (pages 49–52): cognitive demand, and the requirement for students to progress in knowledge, understanding and skills.

In the commonest case scenario teachers make the pragmatic assumption that a class is roughly homogeneous in ability level; and they set a single task which makes the same demands on all the students: an undifferentiated task.

In practice, of course, students interpret the task differently because of their different ability levels; and thus the task becomes differentiated by outcome.

An example of this process would be something like this. The students are studying Tennyson's 'The Brook'. At an appropriate moment the teacher decides that the class should analyse what makes the poem effective. He sets an essay for homework: 'Explain what it is that makes Tennyson's The Brook such a lasting piece of work.' Some of the students produce fairly stock answers which reflect what has been said in class: the rhythm of the words, the pace of the language, the rural picture it paints, the repetition of ideas in new settings, and so on. But some students move the thinking on to look at the acute observation of the natural world, which appeals to a growing 'Green' faction in society; while others begin to talk about 'levels of meaning' in which the flow of the brook and the flow of life somehow interface.

This example shows what passes for differentiation in common parlance. But the point is that, strictly speaking, it is not. The task is not differentiated at all. It does produce a differentiated outcome, but that is not precisely the same thing.

It is difficult to be precise, but observation in classrooms suggests that differentiation by outcome as a result of a single common task, happens on as many as 90 per cent of occasions when tasks are set.

This chapter and the next two challenge the adequacy of this pragmatic approach and put forward some ideas for alternative learning and teaching strategies to make differentiation more meaningful, and in particular they look at ways of building differentiation into tasks from the beginning as a *planned strategy*, not simply relying on outcomes.

Activity 16

Reviewing your strategies for differentiation

Look back over all the tasks you have set in the last term. How many of them were common tasks set to a whole class/set/band?

How exactly did you differentiate for students of different abilities and stages of understanding?

What proportion of these tasks were differentiated other than by outcome?

Some common attempts at differentiation

Of course, most teachers are aware that differentiation in the way described is less than ideal. There are very real pressures – such as pressures of time and ease of marking – which make the ploy an attractive one. But it is possible to find some other approaches which attempt to overcome the problem of 'common' tasks.

Worksheets contain one of the more widespread approaches. Here, teachers often present a series of tasks, each a little more difficult than the previous one. In this way, everyone can complete a basic core of work which is covered by the earlier tasks; but some students can move on at their own pace (within the time-limits allocated) to more tricky work which makes more demands on their knowledge, skills and understanding.

Another form of differentiation which is quite common is to give specific tasks or additional support to the less able students in the class. Sometimes this method consists of quite sophisticated strategies – such as the use of a well-briefed ancillary – and at other times it simply means the teacher has to spend more time with the less able student while the others get on without help.

Sometimes it is suggested that ability grouping of one kind or another does away with the problem. This is a myth. Ability grouping can obviate the more extreme situations of overall spread of ability within the class; but it does not mean that all those within the streamed class will be performing at the same level or have the same needs. There is still a requirement for differentiation other than by outcome in order to match the task to the individual. A key word in differentiation is indeed the word 'individual'. To listen to some political pronounce-ments about teaching and learning one would think that teaching up to forty students the same thing simultaneously is an effective learning strategy. In limited contexts – such as presenting some new material which everyone needs to share – it can be. But that is as far this strategy goes in terms of what might be labelled 'sensitive teaching'.

Another means to differentiation (rather than a method of differentiation) is the provision by the teacher of additional support materials. For example, a teacher may provide resources for slower learners which are easier to read. Or it may be that the most able are given additional material to cover so as to study the common class topic in more depth. This kind of support can aid the process of differentiation, though in itself it is not differentiation.

Sometimes, too, the teacher agrees with the class different outcomes for different students. He or she may agree that some students should present their work in written form (an essay, an exam-style answer) while others put their thoughts onto a tape-recorder or produce a working model. In the same way, teachers expect more from some students in a given period of time than from others. These are all manifestations of attempts at differentiation rather than methods for achieving it. Each has its uses, and individual methods of differentiation are discussed in more detail below.

Investigating differentiation in classrooms

Because of the difficulty of finding widespread good practice in differentiation it was decided to research both the literature of the subject, and also to carry out some research at professional development days to ask a wide sample of teachers about their differentiation practice. This was done in a context of training about teaching strategies for the more able: since it is when dealing with extremes of ability that differentiation practice becomes more critical and teachers pay more attention to it. (Likewise, reference to differentiation for the less able had been mentioned above.) What follows chronicles the outcomes of these processes.

Guidance on differentiation in the literature

The literature of able pupil education is full of exhortations to teachers to increase task demand and strengthen the cognitive content of classroom tasks (Vernon 1977, Wallace 1983, Freeman 1995). There is ample evidence to suggest that this is sound advice (Kerry, 1984). For many teachers the reality of classroom life is that they teach in mixed ability contexts, in primary schools often in mixed age contexts as well. They are presented not only with task-setting for the 'core' group of pupils within the class – sometimes referred to as the middle band – but also a range of pupils of higher and lower ability, some of whom will be at relatively extreme ends of the intellectual continuum. Perhaps for this reason, advice to teachers about task demand has, in recent years, come to be grouped under the broader heading of differentiation. The teacher's skills of differentiation are, it is assumed, aimed more generally at pupils across the intellectual spectrum.

Differentiation rose to prominence on the education agenda after the 1988 Education Act. The ill-fated School Examinations and Assessment Council (SEAC undated) produced a set of guidance books for teachers, one of which identified two methods of differentiation: by task and by outcome. This rather unsophisticated approach occupied just one page of their eighty-eight pages of guidance in the cited work.

Now that all classrooms are being inspected by Ofsted inspectors, and that differentiation is high on their agenda when observing teaching skills, teachers are expected to show a range of skills in differentiating work for pupils. However, this fact epitomises the teacher's dilemma. For, while on the one hand Ofsted inspectors review teachers' differentiation skills when observing teaching, on the other hand the primary Handbook of Inspection (1995) does not contain the word in its index and does not refer explicitly to it in the text. Yet, inevitably, teachers have looked to official publications for guidance about how differentiation should work when well executed by a skillful practitioner. What advice has been available to them?

If Ofsted itself has been coy about setting down its criteria for effective differentiation, then some of its inspectors have been more forthcoming. Thus Laar (1995) in the *Times Educational Supplement* notes that a number of traditional approaches have been in common use:

- ordering the learning complexity of tasks set to pupils;
- devoting additional time to pupils with learning needs;
- grouping by ability;
- providing different (levels of) support material;
- accepting different levels of achievement and modes of presentation by pupils.

He goes on to suggest some additional strategies, notably that pupils in the same class can work on different 'strands' of the subject matter; that classroom assistants are used to support those who work with difficulty; that pupils are encouraged to pursue personal interests within the subject in more depth.

HMI had some views on differentiation in the specific context of teaching the more able. In a review of practice (HMI, 1992) in primary and secondary schools they identified four methods of differentiation:

- by outcome;
- by rate of response;
- by enrichment;
- by setting different tasks.

But they warned that none of these worked unless they were built into the teacher's planning and used with a consciousness of desired outcome. For them, control was a keynote; and they were able to conclude:

> *The strategies were successful when the teacher had determined in advance what the pupil should learn, without excluding scope for originality. Consequently, the fourth strategy, in which differentiation had been built into the scheme of work and the planning of lessons, and in which explicit pathways to higher cognitive and intellectual development had been identified, was almost always associated with good practice.*

(para 38)

This approach, while adding something beyond the SEAC contribution, has some inherent dangers in terms of the extent to which the pre-planning of the teacher (laudable in itself) could, in less competent hands, slip into over-control. Indeed, one such scenario is exemplified by Pollard (1994) in materials relating to the Open University's PGCE course. Pollard describes a primary class in which the social grouping and teaching strategies 'feed' the judgement of the teacher about differentiating work. What develops is the classic case of the self-fulfilling prophecy: in a context of high levels of pupil-pupil collaboration children on high performing tables have access to more correct answers, and children on low performing tables have less access – thus confirming the teachers' views of them as able and less able respectively. While tasks were differentiated, classroom organisation ensured that children could only continue to perform well or badly, and the desired outcomes of progress and improvement were negated.

To contrast with this, the government's favoured think-tank group on primary education produced a paper (Alexander, Rose and Woodhead, 1992) which claimed the exact opposite to be the desired outcome of differentiating classroom work:

> *Standards of education in primary schools will not rise until teachers expect more of their pupils, and, in particular, more of able and disadvantaged children.*

(p32)

Having exhausted themselves with this insight, the remainder of their section on this topic is remarkably unhelpful and unexplicit, concluding:

> *... the best the teacher can do ... is to devise the classroom settings and pupil tasks which give the best chance of success.*

(p32)

Oddly enough, that is probably exactly what most teachers thought they were already trying to do; and they were looking to such prestigious publications to give them ideas and guidance: to no avail as it happened.

By far the most helpful document to come from an 'official' stable has been that from the National Council for Educational Technology (NCET). In this Dickson and Wright (1993) examine differentiation in some detail, identifying that it can come through:

- content
- resource
- task
- outcome
- response
- support.

In a shortened version of this book (Open University, 1996) – designed for one of the most recent courses of initial teacher training and so, presumably, the repository of current wisdom and knowledge for the next generation of teachers – there is a significant discussion of how each of these methods of differentiation might work in practice, with examples from the classroom.

Researching teachers' own methods of differentiation

The consciousness of teachers of the need to differentiate across all classroom situations is due in no small measure to the emphasis placed on this range of strategies by various official pronouncements, as we have seen above. But our initial investigations seemed to suggest that little research had been undertaken to explore systematically either the feelings and collected professional wisdom of teachers about the recommended strategies, or to evaluate the effectiveness of the strategies with one of the key target groups of pupils at whom they are aimed: the more able. In this research we attempted an initial exploration of both of these issues.

We wanted to explore a number of issues:

- whether teachers use the recommended methods of differentiation;
- what happens when they do;

- the extent to which these recommended methods are deemed by teachers to be successful;
- how these methods relate specifically to the teaching of the more able pupils in primary and secondary classes.

With these issues in mind we set out to gather information in two ways. Using opportunity samples of teachers in primary and secondary schools who were attending our in-service courses on teaching the more able, we devised two workshop tasks.

The first workshop task presented small groups of teachers with a list of the fifteen most regularly recommended methods of differentiation culled from the literature. Using a proforma (Table 8), the teachers were asked to discuss and record two ways in which each of the fifteen methods proved successful in practice, and two ways in which they proved unsuccessful. In most cases the workshop members then produced a group-response to the task. Over time we collected a number of these group responses from a variety of schools; we also collected some individual responses in situations where this was more appropriate.

In the second workshop task (Table 9) we asked the staff:
- to articulate their desired outcomes from setting differentiated tasks to groups containing some able pupils;
- to describe a differentiated task they had set and to say why they thought it appropriate;
- to say what problems they had come across in setting differentiated tasks to more able pupils.

By using two different methods for gathering data we hoped to get a detailed and 'rounded' picture of the ways in which differentiation worked, or did not work, and some insight into the reasons. We wanted to move from the theoretical models to some practical experience which could be built into advice for teachers.

Workshop task 1 proved to be an engaging task which teachers enjoyed: they found the debate which it triggered enlightening – in secondary schools this was especially so when carried out in cross-departmental groups. The outcomes were interesting in that what we gained was a substantial insight into the advantages and disadvantages of the fifteen recommended methods of differentiation. These are discussed in some detail in Chapter 9 of this book. But this an appropriate moment at which to try the task for yourself.

Activity 17

Assessing methods of differentiation

Use the proforma from Table 8 to assess your own views of fifteen common methods of differentiation identified by other teachers.

Consider each of the 15 methods in turn, and write down two advantages and two disadvantages for it.

When you have done this, keep your completed proforma, and compare it with the results which you will find in Chapter 9.

What do we want to achieve through differentiation?

Workshop task 2, referred to above, probed the intentions behind differentiation. In the first three chapters of this book there was an analysis of learning intentions: and in using various methods of differentiation it was possible to extend the learning intentions of lessons.

The outcomes from this second task can be seen in Table 10.

Table 8

Methods of differentiation: a proforma

Method of differentiation	Pros	Cons
Using graduated worksheets		
Making available resource packs of additional information		
Asking open questions more often		
Using individual pupil contracts/targets		
Challenging pupils' assumptions and received values		
Increasing the use of support teachers or parent helpers		
Encouraging self-pacing by pupils		
Removing unnecessary repetition (e.g. multiple similar examples to be worked)		
Using homework time for the production of an extended project		
Promoting self-marking/self-criticism by pupils of their work		
Allowing pupils to record responses in different ways, e.g. pictures, cartoons, audiotapes, graphs		
Asking cognitively demanding questions		
Setting tasks with no single correct solution		
Using role play		
Setting tasks with increased thinking demand		

Table 9

Proforma for collecting teachers' views

Differentiating classroom tasks
for able pupils

One of the commonest strategies for dealing with able pupils in the classroom is to set them a task which is differentiated from the tasks set to other pupils.

In this activity we are interested in the criteria for differentiation which teachers use and in the processes of setting differentiated tasks to the more able.

Please write a freehand response to each
of the following questions.

1. When you set a separate differentiated task to more able pupils, what are the outcomes you hope to achieve by doing this? e.g. 'buying some time until other pupils catch up'.

   a. ....

   b. ....

   c. ....

   d. ....

2. Please describe briefly a differentiated task you have set to more able pupils and then say why you thought it was appropriate.

   a. Task: ....

   ....

   b. Why appropriate: ....

   ....

3. What problems do you come across in trying to differentiate tasks or in using a range of differentiated tasks with able pupils in the classroom?

   a. ....

   b. ....

   c. ....

Table 10

Teachers' desired outcomes from differentiated tasks

1. To increase pupils' knowledge/understanding of a particular area of study.
2. To enable pupils to engage in their own research.
3. To increase pupils' skills in self-research/working on their own.
4. To try to get more able pupils to ask questions, e.g. 'Why things happen' and 'What are the facts?'
5. To create a greater need to want to understand our world.
6. To develop confidence and self-reliance.
7. To encourage questioning and problem solving.
8. To challenge the pupils and stretch the more able.
9. To match the task to the able pupil's higher ability.
10. To extend the able pupil's thinking beyond their usual level.
11. To offer pupils the opportunity of a challenge.
12. To widen their knowledge and skills both in breadth and depth of knowledge.
13. To buy time.
14. To produce display work.
15. To complete research which may be passed on to others.
16. To sustain the interest of the pupil.
17. To use the able pupil's time effectively.
18. To prevent boredom setting in.
19. To make the work more satisfying for the pupil involved.
20. To set challenges and push boundaries.
21. To see just how far pupils can be pushed!
22. To develop higher order skills.
23. To allow the able pupil to go into more detail.
24. To allow the able pupil to use vocabulary that is relevant to the task.
25. To allow the able pupil to use or illustrate some recent example of grammar that has been covered in a whole class lesson.
26. To give pupils a chance to express themselves more fully.
27. To give pupils extra knowledge of the subject.
28. To enable pupils to become more self-critical.

Drawing together the themes of this chapter

Differentiation is an important, planned aspect of effective task-setting. It is the way in which tasks can be consciously matched to the individual needs and abilities of students. This in turn enhances the effectiveness of the teacher's learning objectives for lessons. Well differentiated tasks keep students more interested in their work, and lay the foundation for improved progress. Differentiation may indeed be a means of helping to assess and measure progress in learning. The commonest form of differentiation – differentiation by outcome – is, arguably not a genuine method of differentiation at all since it is not 'built in' it is an 'incidental'.

There is too little 'official' guidance about what constitutes effective differentiation; though professional wisdom can throw some light on a wide range of strategies. In the next chapter we take a more detailed look at the fifteen strategies (listed in Table 8 above); and at what teachers have to say about them.

References to Chapter 8

Alexander, R, Rose, J and Woodhead, C (1992) *Curriculum Organisation and Classroom Practice in Primary Schools.* London: DES.

Dickinson, C and Wright, J (1993) *Differentiation: a practical handbook of classroom strategies.* Coventry: NCET.

Freeman, J, Span, P and Wagner, J (1995) *Actualising Talent.* London: Cassell.

HMI (1992) *Education observed: the education of very able children in maintained schools.* London: DES.

Kerry, T (1984) 'Analysing the cognitive demand made by classroom tasks in mixed ability classes' in Wragg, E C (1984) *Classroom Teaching Skills.* London: Croom Helm.

Laar, B (1995) 'An inspector writes' *Times Educational Supplement,* 8.12.95.

Ofsted (1995) *The Ofsted Handbook: Guidance on the Inspection of Nursery and Primary Schools.* London: HMSO.

Open University (1996) *Extracts from NCET: Differentiation.* Milton Keynes: Open University Press.

Pollard, A (1994) 'Coping strategies and the multiplication of differentiation in infant classrooms' in Bourne, J (1994) *Thinking Through Primary Practice.* London: OU/Routledge.

SEAC (undated) *A Guide to Teacher Assessment Pack C: A sourcebook for teacher assessment.* London: Heinemann.

Vernon, P, Adamson, G and Vernon, D (1977) *The Psychology and Education of Gifted Children.* London: Methuen.

Wallace, B (1983) *Teaching Very Able Children.* London: Ward Lock.

Chapter 9

Differentiation in practice: the teachers' perspectives

An overview of the research on methods of differentiation

In the previous chapter it was indicated that, as part of our research into differentiation, we asked a large sample of teachers to reflect on fifteen common methods of differentiation. These were listed in Table 8. The outcome of this process was that, over time and across a variety of primary and secondary schools, we were able to gain a good feel for the ways in which teachers found these different methods usable and useful. We were able, too, to track what the drawbacks to each method were. In contrast to the literature on the subject, the professional wisdom about differentiation was able to pinpoint both the good and the bad features within each method (that is, rather than merely comparing and contrasting one method with another). At the risk of labouring this point it is our intention to set out here the pros and cons of each of the methods investigated, as reported to us by our teacher respondents. This is done most economically in a series of Tables (Tables 11 to 25) below.

Before you go on to study the Tables which follow, read and bear in mind Activity 18. When you have studied the Tables 11 to 25 re-visit Activity 18 and complete it.

Activity 18

Assessing the value of different methods of differentiation

Tables 11 to 25 set out the pros and cons, the strengths and weaknesses, of fifteen methods of differentiation, as teachers in our sample saw them.

Implicit in this analysis is a strategy for how each method can be most appropriately used.

As you read each Table try to answer these questions for each method:

- How would I use this method?
- For what purpose?
- For which groups of students?
- When would I avoid this method?
- How can this method contribute to a balanced programme of differentiation, to provide variety in my lessons?

Table 11

Method 1: Using graduated worksheets

Pros	Cons
■ provides plenty of work for pupils to do	■ able pupils can avoid challenging work
■ uses appropriate language	■ may have restricted outcomes
■ good for re-inforcement	■ is an invidious way of indicating level of work
■ stretches children	■ may not target gifted pupils accurately
■ pupils can work at their own pace	■ may require teacher's support if not understood
■ provides self-pacing	■ limited teacher/pupil interaction results
■ aids organisation of class	■ can be child minding
■ frees teacher to aid individuals	■ some able pupils may not reach more difficult task
■ works well for all levels of ability	■ can cause death by worksheet
■ is an accepted method of matching work to ability	■ can be time consuming

Table 12

Method 2: Making available resource packs of additional information

Pros	Cons
■ encourages children to work with large quantities of data	■ makes extra preparation work for the teacher
■ is useful for extension work	■ is time-consuming
■ develops further knowledge	■ is costly
■ may provide extra stimulation/interest	■ can be more of the same
■ may provide more demanding material	■ may inhibit the less able
■ may provide more open-ended tasks	■ resources may date rapidly
■ can aid pupils at all levels of ability	■ cost limited resources
■ encourages self-learning	■ materials may go missing
■ targets individual interests	■ there may be storage difficulties
■ can be self generating work	■ pupils need direction on how to use them
	■ can produce 'mess' in the work area

Table 13

Method 3: Asking open questions more often

Pros	Cons
■ allows scope for creativity	■ is hard for teacher to do successfully
■ encourages pupil to think more	
■ engages pupil's attention	■ needs preparation
■ is challenging and builds rapport	■ may produce peer group derision
■ is not time-consuming for the teacher	■ is less good for quieter pupils
	■ could take wrong route
■ stretches able orally	■ may be intimidating (especially to those of lower ability)
■ checks understanding	
■ encourages lateral thinking	■ can miss parts of the curriculum
■ stretches the more able	■ less able likely to be limited even more than usual within the mixed ability class
■ enables pupils to express themselves	
	■ is open to misinterpretation
	■ means same pupils volunteer answers

Table 14

Method 4: Using individual contracts/targets

Pros	Cons
■ increases motivation	■ is time-consuming for the teacher
■ leads to precise learning	■ is a paperwork nightmare
■ gives pupil ownership of learning	■ needs constant monitoring
■ sees pupil as an individual	■ needs good record-keeping
■ gives pupil clear goals	■ targets may have to be changed
■ creates challenge	■ targets may be aimed too low/high
■ sets both short- and long-term targets	
	■ means pupil may only work to contract
■ is useful in individual situations	
■ is sometimes useful in group situations	■ can be very proscriptive
	■ labels pupils
■ gives clear expectation of target	■ needs a lot of setting-up time

Table 15

Method 5: Challenging pupils' assumptions and received values

Pros	Cons
■ makes pupil think deeply	■ can undermine parents' values
■ moves pupil on and encourages independent thought	■ causes pupils to feel intimidated
■ develops pupils' own values	■ could be confrontational
■ challenges complacency	■ can knock pupils' confidence
■ encourages creativity	■ could result in alienation
■ sets tasks appropriately	■ may result in criticism being construed negatively
■ broadens the pupils' thoughts	■ increases insecurity for some
■ makes children think and enter into debate	■ may confuse
■ makes pupils reason out their point of view	■ challenges pupils so much that they lose confidence
■ makes pupils think of others' point of view	■ highlights the need for honesty

Table 16

Method 6: Increasing the use of support teachers or parent helpers

Pros	Cons
■ encourages the child	■ is expensive
■ increases motivation and enthusiasm	■ may have training implications
■ gives more adult support	■ some pupils don't like individual support
■ broadens parents' understanding	■ some pupils become dependent upon individual support
■ can help meet individual needs and can only serve to help them	■ adult may not be sufficiently skilled
■ releases main class for teacher	■ parents may have set ideas
■ gives an opportunity for conversation with adults	■ conflicting advice/confusion may result
■ is also excellent for less able	■ draws unnecessary attention to able pupils
■ gives an extra pair of hands	■ the teacher must be able to select the helper
■ introduces new skills into the classroom	■ raises issues of safety

Table 17

Method 7: Encouraging self-pacing by pupils

Pros	Cons
■ is an efficient use of time	■ can be abused
■ makes pupils independent	■ needs a lot of monitoring
■ helps pupils learn how to learn	■ might be their weak area
■ takes pressure off teacher	■ encourages some pupils to 'slack'
■ develops expectations of self	■ allows pupils to move on without
■ teaches time-management skills	knowledge/understanding/skills
■ allows pupils to learn at a comfortable rate, and removes the idea of competition	■ gives scope to those under-achieving because of lack of effort
■ gives pupils greater ownership	■ is time-consuming to monitor
■ allows pupils to realise their own ability	■ relies on keeping a challenging pace – pupils need skills and motivation
■ is particularly useful for routine/sequence work	■ could encourage children to rush work
	■ needs skills of self-motivation
	■ requires appropriate skills from teacher

Table 18

Method 8: Removing unnecessary repetition (e.g. multiple similar exercises to be worked)

Pros	Cons
■ saves time to be spent on harder tasks	■ removes chance of revision and consolidation
■ stops boredom	■ means teacher has to prepare extra work
■ allows pupils to increase their knowledge of other topics	■ results in boredom
■ leaves more time for progress	■ denies opportunities for re-inforcement
■ removes disruption	
■ sustains motivation	
■ creates more curriculum time for different, challenging work	

Table 19

Method 9: Using homework time for an extended project

Pros	Cons
■ is motivational	■ is hard because of lack of books in disadvantaged homes
■ encourages initiative	■ leads to pupil burn-out
■ uses home/town library resources	■ is open to abuse
■ is self-pacing	■ needs to be shaped by teacher
■ allows for creativity	■ can be repetitive
■ improves study skills	■ may mean student feels 'left to it'
■ allows pupils to pursue their own ideas	■ may falter because of unsuitable learning environment
■ gives pupil the ability to set own aims, goals	■ means asking: who is really doing the work at home?
■ encourages pupil to use many areas outside school to gain knowledge and information	■ may be resented
■ makes extra time available	■ may put pupil under pressure
	■ might lead to pupil not working in school

Table 20

Method 10: Promoting self-marking/self-criticism by pupils of their work

Pros	Cons
■ demonstrates deeper levels of thought	■ is easier for objective tasks
■ focuses attention	■ requires a good mark scheme
■ promotes responsibility	■ is open to abuse, cheating
■ allows for analysis of own skills	■ doesn't relieve teacher of need to see work
■ develops evaluative skills and recognition of standards	■ may falter because pupils tend to under-estimate their own standard
■ teaches about targets	■ may miss out some relevant criteria
■ provides a basis of discussion of what is 'success'	■ may be hampered by modesty
■ allows pupils to celebrate and evaluate their own work	■ can be shallow
■ promotes self-analysis: how they can improve; what they need to concentrate on	■ may fail if pupils think they can perform skill/task already
■ if monitored through a central register, can be valuable	■ is time-consuming
	■ is non-productive for those pupils with a negative self-image

Table 21

Method 11: Allowing pupils to record responses in different ways, e.g. pictures, cartoons, audio tape, graphs

Pros	Cons
■ gives scope for different talents	■ encourages avoidance techniques
■ is quicker	■ falls foul of expense of resources
■ provides novelty value	■ means that teacher may need to develop new skills
■ gives freedom of expression	■ means pupils may have to develop the necessary skills
■ develops knowledge of working with a variety of media	■ is time-consuming
■ encourages self-motivation	■ is difficult to mark
■ develops a variety of talents	■ is expensive
■ aids analysis	■ may affect literacy development
■ re-inforces learning	■ might lead to 'ducking' more rigorous work
■ gives students some control	■ may mean pupils don't always stretch themselves to try other ways
	■ is not always challenging

Table 22

Method 12: Asking cognitively demanding questions

Pros	Cons
■ re-inforces knowledge	■ makes it difficult for the pupil to work alongside less able friends
■ reaches those who need targeting	■ may make some pupils feel threatened
■ develops pupils' own understanding	■ is time-consuming
■ stretches pupils	■ may demotivate less able
■ helps reasoning skills	■ may pressurise the more able
■ shows there are no clear answers	■ requires increased preparation of demanding questions by teacher
■ gets pupils' thinking focused and directed	■ requires increased level of teacher's skill and knowledge
■ aids general knowledge and study skills	■ could have negative effect on child with low self-esteem
■ challenges the pupils	■ may not elicit hoped for level of response
■ develops evaluation techniques	

Table 23

Method 13: Setting tasks with no single correct solution

Pros	Cons
■ is realistic, teaches about life	■ may be depressing
■ encourages creativity	■ is perhaps available only to part of the class
■ encourages self-motivation	■ becomes meaningless?
■ means pupils are forced to substantiate claims	■ can provide a sense of existential despair
■ means pupils can achieve their own standards and work to improve upon them	■ needs more resources
■ can provide creative, thoughtful outcomes	■ makes more work for teachers
■ produces a variety of solutions	■ is difficult to mark
■ encourages creative thinking	■ is frustrating for pupils
■ allows open-ended learning opportunities	■ some pupils need more guidance
■ makes pupils think	■ can be a difficult concept for pupils

Table 24

Method 14: Using role play

Pros	Cons
■ encourages empathetic thinking	■ means shy, nervous pupils hide
■ encourages social interaction	■ can be mechanical
■ allows learning to take place in a more relaxed atmosphere	■ is time-consuming to set up properly
■ takes pupil beyond the normal range of responses	■ threatens some pupils
■ leads to holistic learning	■ produces problems of control
■ gives opportunities for different interpretation	■ is too difficult a concept for some pupils
■ develops life skills	
■ puts learning into practice	
■ offers an alternative way into a topic	
■ gives variety	

Table 25

Method 15: Setting tasks with increased thinking demand

Pros	Cons
■ means bright children are often intrigued by the challenge	■ causes problems with assessment
■ stimulates	■ requires tasks to be structured
■ stretches those who can think for themselves and be creative	■ can be demotivating for less able
	■ inhibits those who need guidance
■ promotes problem solving and extension	■ may promote daydreaming
■ motivates	■ means increased preparation for teacher
	■ demands teacher skills
	■ means lack of understanding by pupil may 'turn them off'

We believe that the findings from this research are unique in two important ways. They demonstrate an insight into the thinking of teachers themselves which is lacking in most of the literature; and they demonstrate a subtlety of approach to each method of differentiation which is certainly not a feature of official publications and pronouncements. To illustrate this we can return to our four research questions, outlined earlier on pages 99–100.

Do teachers use the 'recommended' methods of differentiation?

The answer is affirmative: but they use them with caution, and not uncritically. Teachers do not find them to be blanket solutions to the problems of matching in the classroom, and they are certainly not always successful, even with more able pupils. For each method quoted the 'cons' are finely balanced with the 'pros' – and there is an emphasis on the need to take contextual factors into account when deciding whether the method is appropriate. A good example of this is in the use of Method 1: Using graduated worksheets (Table 11). The positive view is that this method is effective if used sparingly, to aid students' self-pacing and to bring about a match of task to student; indeed it may help class management and it has the advantage that it gives teachers confidence precisely because it is a 'recommended' method. But the negative aspects of this method are considerable: it does not guarantee a 'match' between task and pupil and may even miss the opportunity of challenge for the more able. There is a danger of boredom ('death by worksheet'). For the teacher there is a resource implication relating to extra preparation time and also monitoring of a different set of student work. Some students may find the process divisive in highlighting their ability and alienating them from peers. Thus, even when the fundamental 'recommended' aim of matching is achieved, the overall educational value of this method may, in certain contexts, be somewhat wide of the mark.

What happens when teachers use the 'recommended' methods of differentiation?

As we have seen, teachers do use recommended methods of differentiation even though they treat them with a degree of scepticism. This process has been described above in relation to the first method in Table 11: using graduated worksheets. The same picture emerges for the remaining fourteen methods listed there.

Thus we see that the use of additional resources is seen by teachers to be useful because it extends the scope of any given topic, especially for the more able, providing increased task demand, improved opportunity for open-ended study and a close match with reading ability. The drawbacks are in terms of production time for the teacher, limitations of cost, and the danger of the work becoming mere extension rather than enrichment. In the same way, asking more open-ended questions would appear to be a logical differentiation strategy for use in classes of mixed ability or those containing able students; and it is. Such a ploy can encourage creativity and promote lateral thinking; all students will be challenged and may improve their skills of articulation of knowledge. But the down-side is that it requires considerable skill from the teacher, it may disadvantage slower learners, and even some more able pupils may find the process of challenge daunting.

Learning contracts, too, have their pros and cons. The individualisation of work can be a gain; and so can the potential for pacing the work of youngsters more appropriately. Yet formal contracts represent administrative labour and the tracking of progress can be time-consuming; some students don't like their levels of ability to be identified in this way, either. Similarly, just as asking open-ended questions is challenging, so the challenging of students' assumptions may be viewed negatively by parents or be seen by students themselves as threatening; and this despite the best intentions of encouraging deeper thought and more extended reasoning skills.

Some of the recommended methods are, in practical terms, more under control of the teacher than others. Using support staff and parents may prove valuable in allowing real needs to be targeted and in terms of student encouragement; but the problem in many schools is that such help can be expensive and often does not exist. Even where it does exist it requires careful management. So can self-pacing by more able students – apparently undemanding of resource – be used effectively? Yes, it can: it provides the student with a greater ownership of learning, with time-management skills and with motivation, possibly. But even here teachers are aware that the more idle can fail to benefit from this option and underachievement may actually be encouraged.

Even with a method of differentiation as simple as removing the unnecessary repetition of multiple examples (e.g. of maths problems relating to a topic the student has already understood) there is dispute about the efficacy. While this can be seen as a way of gaining time for more worthwhile activities, some teachers favour the multiple examples as a means of revision and re-inforcement. But if opinion is divided on this, homework is even more contentious as a means of differentiating work by setting extended projects from which more able pupils may have opportunities to benefit. For some able youngsters this may be seen as an opportunity for extension, providing motivation and an outlet for interest, as well as a chance to gain extra knowledge against an assessment target. But many able students simply resent being expected to do more work than their peers; they may not have adequate support and resources at home to allow proper benefit to accrue, or may be oversupported or pushed too hard by ambitious parents.

While teachers are very aware of the time pressures on them and might be expected to favour students' self-marking and self-criticism as one means of tackling the marking chore, they are aware of drawbacks. For some students, it might represent a real chance to become analytical and independent, but for others it is a chance to cheat, to over-assess or under-play their skills. But if self-marking is ambiguous as a means to differentiate work, even for the more able, then allowing students to record their responses to classroom tasks in various media is even more problematic. This method depends on stretched resources, requires specific skills in students which they may not have, and provides the teacher with increased problems of assessment for work on the same topic in varying formats. So the values – motivation through variety, student-centredness, freedom of expression, for example – can be outweighed in some circumstances.

Asking cognitively demanding questions is a commonly recommended method of differentiating classroom work for the more able and – for all students – may help reasoning skills, contribute an element of curiosity, and demonstrate that to some questions there are no clear answers. But in a mixed ability group the process can be divisive: and even the able may be demoralised if the teacher fails to pitch the demand accurately. In the same way, setting tasks with no single correct solution, or tasks with increased thinking demand, can be a double-edged sword for all the same reasons.

Finally, a common suggestion is to use role play: this may give opportunities for more affective responses to knowledge, providing useful life-skills. Its value is limited, though, in that many students are too shy and vulnerable to respond, and the class management implications may stretch the teacher's own skills.

To what extent are the 'recommended' methods of differentiation deemed by teachers to be successful?

The brief review of teachers' assessments of various methods of differentiation (above), has again stressed that each method must be separately reviewed and weighed for both its strength and weakness within the teaching context in which it is selected. This is the fundamental and recurrent insight of this research, and the feature which marks it out from most of the 'official' guidance on methods of differentiation.

How do the 'recommended' methods of differentiation relate specifically to the teaching of more able students in primary and secondary schools?

To answer this question it is appropriate to turn back to the data summarised in Table 10 in Chapter 8 (page 104). Table 10 told us what teachers hoped to achieve through differentiation for able pupils. The salient points were as follows.

Differentiation is about individual challenge: increasing knowledge, skills and understanding. This involves getting students to ask themselves the all-important 'why?' questions, and to solve problems. Differentiation is also about using time effectively: eliminating boredom, pushing back the boundaries of knowledge, capturing interest, practising language skills. Part of that process is the inculcation of study skills and, alongside that, to give a self-critical confidence and sure-footedness to learning.

Summary

Differentiation has been the watchword of the 1990s, and has taken its place among the key criteria for effective classroom practice. Yet much of the advice on this subject has originated in official publications which have, it is suggested, lacked the critical edge of practitioner expertise. In our research we found both primary and secondary teachers struggling to carry out the 'recommendations' of official pronouncements; their strategies have embraced all the main methods of differentiation: of content, resource, task, outcome, response and support. But the practitioners have found that there are subtleties of procedures and strategy which have not been, to date, catered for in the literature. This chapter has attempted to reveal some of these.

Chapter 10

How differentiation helps

Introduction

In this last chapter of the trio on differentiation we move on to look at how differentiation can be used in order to maximise the learning of students in the classroom. To do this I have taken an example from Key Stage 2, from the science curriculum, and from the section on Living Things. But first, it is important to have some background about the students and the task.

Background

The set of differentiated tasks described below formed part of the outcome of a study of living things with a year-group of about sixty-five Year 6 students in a suburban primary school. The students were housed in a large open-plan teaching area, which was well furnished but rather short on facilities (the area had been newly built and was not yet fully equipped). Organisation was mixed ability; a number of students had mild learning difficulties, one was statemented; but at the other extreme of the ability range there were several very able students. The two teachers worked either separately or together, according to need; and there was an ancillary who helped the statemented student. On this occasion, one teacher provided the lead for a series of lessons spread over one week and totalling about six hours of classroom time on the theme of Living Things. She chose to start the work using Owls as the stimulus.

(THOSE WHO WOULD LIKE TO DO SO MAY WISH TO PURSUE THE CONTENT OF PART OF THIS LESSON SEQUENCE WHICH IS USED IN THE COMPANION BOOK IN THIS SERIES: *QUESTIONING AND EXPLAINING IN CLASSROOMS*. HOWEVER, IT IS NOT ESSENTIAL TO AN UNDERSTANDING OF THE POINT MADE HERE TO PURSUE THIS CROSS-REFERENCE. THE LEARNING OBJECTIVES FOR THIS LESSON SEQUENCE ARE DISCUSSED IN CHAPTER 1 OF THIS BOOK.)

The short sequence of lessons was planned to take account of the points made earlier in this book about formulating effective learning objectives. Figure 9, therefore, sets out the planning for the sequence using a proforma very similar to the one described earlier in Figure 3 (page 25).

OVERALL SESSION PLAN (4 lessons)

CURRICULUM AREA: Science Key Stage 2 Year 6
Life Processes & Living Things
Living things in their environment

INTENTIONS:

- To introduce & give insight into some key concepts: adaptation, habitat, territory, eco-system
- To link the work with previous learning e.g. food webs & food chains
- To give a context to the work within scientific processes: observing, hypothesising, using data and evidence, drawing conclusions
- To link scientific and aesthetic responses

RELATION TO KEY STAGE 2 NC:

The work will be centred in Section 5 – Living things and their environment. The students have been on a visit to a nature trail which illustrated 5a,5b. The knowledge will be extended to 5c, 5d. This will be achieved by using and reinforcing processes in Investigative Science i.e. 1c,d,e, 2b and 3a,b,c. The students will look at the interactions between owls and hedgerows to examine scientific concepts. They will work across subject boundaries into art, English, with an aesthetic appreciation of the objects of study (see National Curriculum English KS2 Writing 2a,b; Speaking and listening 1a; and art 7a,b.

CONTENT LESSON BY LESSON – OUTLINE:

1. Observation, deduction – concept of adaptation – these reinforced using pre-prepared worksheets
2. Habitat (including different kinds of adaptation); ideas of territory and the eco-system. Digestion in owls – experiments, hypotheses, evidence and conclusions
3. Aesthetic responses: science and the arts. Owl poems. Start of graded tasks
4. Compiling of draft work into finished products for 'Our book of Owls'.

Intended outcomes:
- A record of personal learning
- A class book about owls.

DIFFERENTIATION:

To be achieved mainly through a series of differentiated tasks targeted at specific students' needs and levels of ability.

KEY RESOURCES:

Stuffed owl; specially prepared worksheets on adaptation; owl proforma for sketching; resource materials for each of the tasks to be set; task cards.

TEACHING & LEARNING METHODS:

Whole class work for initial information and stimulus.
Individual work for recording.
Individualised and group work for carrying out tasks.

CURRICULUM LINKS:

Varied from one student to another, but including links with art, poetry, literature, and mathematics.

PLANNED ASSESSMENT STRATEGIES:

Feedback through question and answer including higher order questions.
Shared, differentiated tasks.
Final contributions to 'Our book of Owls' by individuals.

EVALUATION:

(To be completed after the sessions).

DIAGRAM OF LESSON CONTENT

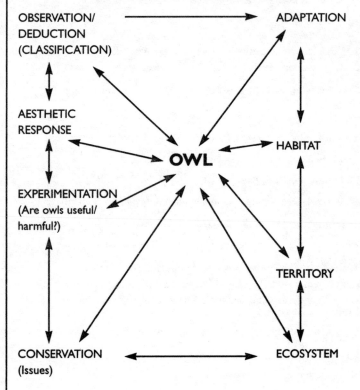

LESSON 1

Lesson objectives (knowledge, skills, understanding, attitudinal, affective)

At the end of this session the students will be able to:

1. Observe acutely and articulate the value of observation
2. Deduce intelligently and articulate the value of deduction
3. Understand the concept of adaptation
4. Draw conclusions based on evidence
5. Enjoy looking at the stuffed owl, and at the scientific processes

Outlines of content & sequence

Solve owl riddle

Observe specimen

See: characteristics of its eyes, ears, bill, legs, feet, claws, feathering

Deduce: kills for a living – how? when? where? what?

Creature does not exist in isolation – ADAPTED to its surroundings

Definition

Relationship with other learning

Link with nature trail visit. Drawing from life.

Materials & resources

Stuffed owl. Owl pictures (various media) Riddle cards. Worksheets.

Teaching and learning methods

Whole class stimulus. Questioning to draw out skills, understandings.

Tasks to be set / methods of differentiation

Drawing from life. Using drawing to illustrate adaptation.

Student assessment

To be achieved through questioning and responses to tasks set

Lesson evaluation

(To be completed after the lesson)

LESSON 2

Lesson objectives (knowledge, skills, understanding, attitudinal, affective)

At the end of this session the students will be able to:

1. Understand and define habitat
2. Understand additional kinds of adaptation
3. Explain ecosystem
4. React to owls and other creatures in a variety of ways – scientific & aesthetic

Outlines of content & sequence

Recap lesson 1. Observe: hedgerow – height – long, narrow corridor, effect of this on habitat size, variety of shrubs etc. involved, undergrowth, variety of other wildlife involved.

Deduce: varied food supply. How plentiful? What factors affect this? Vulnerability – human disturbance, farming methods. Type of area used. Territory/ habitat – differences. Link territory, habitat, food chains.

Relationship with other learning

See lesson 1.

Materials & resources

Hedgerow mock-up. Worksheet – what scientists do.

Teaching and learning methods

Whole class – shared data. Question and answer; didactic – but aimed at higher order thinking

Tasks to be set / methods of differentiation

Worksheet for reinforcement.

Student assessment

Through feedback.

Lesson evaluation

(To be completed after the lesson)

LESSON 3

Lesson objectives (knowledge, skills, understanding, attitudinal, affective)

At the end of this session the students will be able to:

1. Recall concepts: habitat, territory, adaptation
2. Explain how scientists observe, guess, test, draw conclusions
3. Apply the foregoing to understanding owl digestions
4. Understand how to gather and use data about owl feeding
5. Link knowledge of owls to examples of owl poetry, literature

Outlines of content & sequence

Explain owl digestive system and reasons for it
Pellets
Identification charts for pellet contents
Some exploded pellets
Worksheet for data recording explained
Equipment for dissection of pellets
Two owl poems

Relationship with other learning

See previous plans

Materials & resources

Pellets
Examples of dissected pellets
Dissecting equipment
Hygiene equipment
Worksheets; texts of poems to be read

Teaching and learning methods

Some didactic introduction. Question and answer. Hands-on experimental work. Recording findings. Listening carefully to poetry.

Tasks to be set / methods of differentiation

Students will have the chance to dissect a pellet; and to try writing some owl poetry. In any leftover time they will begin the graded tasks – individually or in assigned groups – that will lead to 'Our book of Owls'. Differentiation in the last will be through careful assignment of students to cognitively graded tasks, with options to move on when they have achieved their own first goals.

Student assessment

By quality of outcome

Lesson evaluation

(To be completed after the lesson)

LESSON 4

Lesson objectives (knowledge, skills, understanding, attitudinal, affective)

At the end of this session the students will be able to:
1. Contribute an entry to 'Our book of Owls'
2. Apply all the scientific concepts for the course by applying it to the set task
3. Complete one task well at their own level, and maybe move on
4. Have enjoyed the sessions on owls and scientists
5. Work collaboratively to achieve a shared goal

Outlines of content & sequence

Personal work on graded tasks (shown below)

Relationship with other learning

Continued inter-disciplinary approach, with art, literature and mathematics included in the theme

Materials & resources

Task cards. Equipment related to each task card. Class resource collection to aid personal work.

Teaching and learning methods

Mainly group work, though some individuals may complete some work individually.
Collaborative product for the shared outcome – the owl book.

Tasks to be set / methods of differentiation

Tasks graded as shown; students allocated to appropriate task groups

Student assessment

Through task outcomes

Lesson evaluation

(To be completed after the lesson)

Figure 9 – Planning for a sequence of lessons on Living Things – Owls

A brief comment on lesson content

The outline content of the lessons is shown in Figure 9, and for the present purpose there is little need to elaborate on the information provided. What was important for the teacher was to determine effective lesson outcomes. She needed to discover the extent of student learning, to monitor what had and had not been learned effectively (feedback), to set meaningful tasks to this end, and to match the tasks – as far as possible in a large class group – to individual need. All of these intentions are in line with what has been discussed in Chapters 4 to 7 earlier in this book.

Setting differentiated tasks

To this end the teacher decided to set a series of differentiated tasks. She was aware that she needed to set some tasks for the less able, and some for the more able, and that she needed to have a variety of tasks which would extend the learning of specific students in specific directions. These judgements came out of her knowledge of the student group as individuals. She therefore set about devising a range of tasks. However, she felt strongly that a class theme like this should have a flavour of co-operative enterprise about it. In other words, she wanted all the students to feel that they had actually contributed to a shared outcome which could bind the work together for everyone, as well as completing their individual portions of work. For this reason she planned that all the task outcomes should be filed in a special folder entitled "Our book of Owls" which could be put into the class library and be shared with other classes as appropriate.

Given these overall intentions, the class teacher set about devising the series of tasks which would be shared among the students. The following paragraphs describe those tasks in as much detail as is necessary to give the tenor of them.

Owl level 1
DESIGN A COVER

Design a cover for a book about owls.

Make the main feature of your cover an imaginative picture of an owl – the pictures on this card are meant to start you thinking. Come up with some ideas of your own!

Include the title in the cover design:
Our book of Owls

Your cover should be A4 size, this way up →

Make your cover on a sheet of card OR mount it on card when it is finished.

Owl level 2
OWL FOOD CHAIN

The owl is a predator and so it is at the top of its food chain.

Make a neat diagram of a Little Owl's food chain.

- Do this on plain A4 paper and use a line guide when you write
- Put a heading: FOOD CHAIN OF A LITTLE OWL
- Draw the food chain carefully
- Label all the creatures and plants you draw
- IF YOU HAVE TIME . . . Colour the finished diagram with PALE colours e.g. water colour wash.

Owl level 3

OWL CARTOON

Imagine you are the editor of a magazine about birds.

You want to explain to young children how owls live.

You decide to do it by using a series of cartoon pictures and captions (look at the example).

- Draw and caption a series of cartoons explaining how an owl lives.

Owl level 4

OWL POEMS

Look at the printed sheets. Read the poem called TOWN OWL and the one called DISTURBANCES.

Think about what these poems mean.

- On a sheet of lined paper put the title: Owl Poems.
- Now say which of the poems you liked best.
- Now go on and explain why you made this choice.

(When you are writing say which words or sentences in the poem you liked or did not like; say whether the poets do or don't like owls; tell us which bits of the poems you liked most.)

Owl level 5

OWLS AND HEDGEROWS

Owls depend on hedgerows.

1. On a piece of plain A4 paper [this way up > ⬚] draw a
   diagram (sketch) of a hedgerow like the one below. Put in all
   the things you can think of that grow in a hedgerow.

2. Label all the things you have drawn, like this:
   - ■ oak   ■ tree layer
   - ■ hawthorn   ■ hedge layer
   - ■ grass   ■ undergrowth

3. On the diagram labelled 'Improving the habitat for owls' carry
   out these tasks:
   - ■ The diagram shows a big field. How could the farmer
     divide the field into four to make the best habitat for owls?
     (Draw your answer onto the sheet.)
   - ■ Answer the questions on the bottom of the sheet.

   i) In what other ways could the farmer make his field attractive to
      owls (for example, how could he encourage an owl to nest?)
   ii) Why might a farmer find it useful to have an owl around the
       farm?

Owl level 6

KINDS OF OWL IN BRITAIN

1. How many kinds of owl can be seen in the British Isles? (Use
   the CDs/books to find the information.)
2. (On A4 lined paper) Make a neat list of the kinds of owls you
   discover.
3. Each of these kinds of owl lives in a slightly different kind of
   habitat and eats slightly different food. Make a table like the one
   below to show the type of owl, its habitat and its food:

Type of owl	Habitat	Food
Little owl		
Barn owl		
(and so on)		

4. By looking at the books, can you work out ways in which each kind of owl has adapted differently from the others? (Here is a clue: think about things like size, colour, shape . . .)
   Write your answers below the table you have drawn.

Owl level 7

OWL PELLETS

Ask the teacher for some contents from an owl's pellet and an identification chart.

Try to identify what creatures the owl has eaten.

Make a list of the creatures you identify.

Write this list on a sheet of A4 lined paper:
- Put the heading: CONTENTS OF AN OWL' S PELLET
- Make a list
- Write a few lines about your findings (for example: were the remains hard to identify; did you find anything that surprised you? and so on).

Owl level 8

OWL EATING

On the sheets there is information about food taken by a Tawny Owl

- in the country
- in the rural outskirts of London
- in Holland Park (a city area).

1. Write two or three paragraphs setting down the differences in the owl's feeding habits between the three places.
2. In each case, gives some reasons why you think these owls were feeding like this in the three different habitats.

Owl level 9

COMPARING OWLS

On the sheets you will find information about:

- the food taken by a Tawny Owl living in a woodland habitat AND
- the food taken by a Barn Owl living in a farmland habitat.

Look at this carefully and then answer these questions (write the answers on A4 lined paper).

1. How many reasons can you think of to explain the differences between the feeding of the two owls?
2. Would it be possible for a Barn Owl and a Tawny Owl to live in the same territory? Write down your reasons for giving your answer.

Owl level 10

OWL ARITHMETIC

(You will need a calculator for this task)

(Write your answers on A4 lined paper)

Five pairs of Barn Owls live in one square mile. Between them they capture 24 000 rodents a year.

1. What is a rodent? (use a dictionary if you don't know)
2. How many rodents does ONE of the birds take in a year?
3. How many rodents does ONE bird take in a month?
4. At what time of the year are they likely to take most rodents? Why?
5. Here are some facts about rodents; read them and then try to answer the question:
   - A rodent breeds when it is six months old
   - A pair of rodents produces a litter of young every two months from then on
   - Each litter contains 10 young

   If there are two young rodents on the owl's territory on 1st January 1995, how many do you think there will be on 31st December 1995 if none are killed?

6. If there were no owls, what would happen to the number of rodents on the owl's territory? (Think carefully about the answer.)

Examining the role of differentiation through a classroom example

To date this chapter has described a teacher's planning, the formulation of learning objectives, and her task-setting strategies, leading to the devising of a series of differentiated tasks for a group of Year 6 students. We have now looked at some examples of those tasks. This may be an opportune moment to tackle Activity 19.

Activity 19

Critiquing a teacher's differentiation strategies

From the background information given in this chapter, and the task descriptions provided, examine the effectiveness of the teacher's attempt to differentiate work for this class.

Specifically, try to answer the following questions:

- How effective do you think are the plans the teacher has made for dealing with the range of ability within the class?
- What problems do you think the teacher might have encountered in setting up this sequence of differentiated tasks?
- How effective would these tasks have been in providing information about individual student understanding of the topic?
- From what you can deduce, what additional tasks might the teacher have had to consider, or what other factors might she have had to take into account?
- How important do you think was the element of co-operative work which she introduced into the lesson?
- What would you have done differently?
- Could she have set 'one task for all'? If not, why not?
- As a fellow professional, what elements in this teacher's approach do you particularly warm to or admire?

Tracking, and reporting on, differentiated tasks

Differentiation inevitably means that task-setting becomes a more complicated process. It is for this reason that it is even more important than usual (see Chapter 6) for teachers to maintain good records not only of what tasks are set and to whom, but to include notes on the outcomes of the learning for individual students and for the class as a whole.

In this section we look briefly at some methods of keeping track of the outcomes of differentiated tasks and obtaining feedback about student learning. Four possible methods are described and evaluated.

1. Small group tutoring

One of the methods now in-built into the National Literacy Strategy is for teachers to spend some time with small groups of students performing a common task, while other students are intent on other, individual, tasks. This small group tutoring session is designed so that teachers can gain feedback on the learning of the group, can probe the failures of learning, can probe and extend learning, and can record (make simple notes on) what has been achieved and what still needs to be done. This methodology is useful as far as it goes. Since it is a group activity it may not uncover all the problems of individuals, nor indeed all their achievements. It does depend on a high degree of class control since other students must be gainfully occupied. Time for this activity can be quite limited in most classrooms. Nevertheless, as one strategy among many, it should be in the teacher's armoury.

2. Individual tutoring

This is designed so that a teacher can gain a quite detailed insight into how students are progressing. Many schools now timetable some time into the school term so that teachers can spend short sessions with individuals to check on, and guide, progress. The idea is very sound: in the best of all worlds, perhaps it should be a common occurrence. Many teachers would claim that individual tutoring happens, but they probably think of it as an in-class phenomenon taking only a few seconds. The more sustained conversation of 10 to 30 minutes is, however, a more demanding affair for both parties. The real issue here is time, unless it is programmed into the timetable. If it does take place, there should be some systematic, shared log of the outcomes.

3. Maintaining a learning log

A useful and increasingly widespread ploy is for students to be asked to maintain a learning log – that is, to record in some kind of diary a reflective account of how their learning is progressing. This method utilises the principle of metacognition. It has plenty of value – once students have been trained in the process, and the habit, by the teacher. The big advantage is that the student is doing the recording, and the teacher has a tangible record which can be taken away and perused at any convenient time, used at Open Evening and so on. It has a built-in flexibility which does not apply to the previous two strategies, but time still needs to be put aside for it.

4. Peer appraisal

An alternative strategy is for students' work to be subject to scrutiny by their peers. In an earlier chapter (Chapter 7) I described the compilation of a Greek newspaper by a primary class. The arbiters of 'quality' in this instance were the 'editors' – three students appointed to that role. They decided whether writing or pictures were 'good enough' to be included. This method is not a substitute for teacher appraisal and recording. It does reflect the reality of life, however: in the world outside school it is peer appraisal that often counts. The danger might be in the maturity of the students to make judgements, and in the danger of sensitive individuals feeling threatened by the process. It represents a useful, occasional, device for monitoring outcomes from tasks, but not one to be adopted lightly or for prolonged periods.

Activity 20

Considering monitoring and recording methods for differentiated tasks

Look back over the four methods described in this section for monitoring and recording the outcomes of differentiated tasks. How well would each work in your own situation?

Have you tried each one? If there is any you have not tried, find an opportunity to put it to the test and evaluate for yourself.

What other methods do you/could you use? What are the comparative strengths and weakness of these?

So, let us try to draw together some of the thoughts about tracking and recording progress of students through differentiated tasks. A range of strategies is open to teachers; but the use and frequency of those strategies must be monitored to ensure an appropriate balance. Strategies are likely to be effective when they increase teacher-student interaction. An eye must be kept to ensure that, whatever strategies are used, they do not end up by diminishing teaching time significantly. Assessment and appraisal are a part of the learning process – well used a very significant part – by they are not a substitute for other approaches to learning and teaching. While monitoring is in progress for some students, others must be gainfully employed. Where students are given increased freedom to control their own learning (e.g. through the maintenance of learning logs) there must not be loop-holes which allow them opportunities for work avoidance or slowing their own progress. The balance of work for all students between whole class, group work and individualised modes, must be properly maintained. The use of para-professionals to carry out some support tasks in relation to this monitoring process may need to be considered.

Finally, some thought needs to be given to devising some form of written record for a series of differentiated tasks like the one on Living Things described earlier in this chapter. This, then, becomes your last Activity.

Activity 21

Devising written recording procedures for a differentiated task

Look back over the sequence of 'Owl' related tasks described in this chapter. Devise a written record for this. Your record must include:

- a way of indicating what the tasks are/ your learning intentions for them;
- a way of identifying their demand or cognitive level;
- a note of who did which task(s);
- a means for describing achievement in relation to each task;
- a means for identifying future targets for each student/group.

Chapter 11

Conclusion: a rationale for classroom learning

The processes of teaching and learning are not value-free. It is, therefore, inevitable that this book of teaching skills has proposed values about why, how and what students should learn.

Learning is central to what happens in classrooms, and is the main purpose of education. Teaching is the means by which learning takes place. Like the Social Constructivists, this manual has also emphasised that interaction is often essential to effective learning, though that is not to say that all learning has to be carried out exclusively in a social context. Self-learning is a valid methodology.

What this book has tried to put across, too, is that learning can take place effectively only when the intentions for that learning are clear – clear to the teacher, but clear also to the learner. Learning objectives matter first and foremost because they provide the platform on which purposeful activity is predicated. They will, in addition, provide a measure by which evaluation and accountability can operate: but these are secondary considerations. Every teacher should be able to formulate learning objectives in the five domains identified in this manual, and should use them as markers for student progress. Recording that progress is a proper professional activity. Again, recording is part of the external evaluation and accountability process: but it should be first and foremost a part of the teacher's personal professionalism to evaluate and record.

In recent years, external agencies have played up the accountability issue; but my belief is that – as professionals – we should hold it dearer than any external agency does. There is a nice story which illustrates this.

An old saddle-maker took on an apprentice. The boy was good at his job and learned well. His skills were potentially beyond those of his master. The boy served out his apprenticeship, and the time was coming for him to make his final test-piece before setting up as a craftsman in his own right. The old man watched him work, with great pride for he had taught him all he knew. But as he watched, the boy drove one nail home just short of true. It was on the underside of the saddle and would be covered by a fold of leather in the finished work. As the boy worked, the old man put his hand on his arm. 'Why didn't you draw that nail and replace it?' he asked. 'No-one will see it', replied the boy. 'No, but one person will always know the work is less than perfect', said the old man, 'and will you be satisfied with that?'

As professionals we should believe in accountability, but as part of our personal integrity.

So we set the learning objectives of our lessons because that is how learning can best operate. Once set, we have to try to deliver the lessons we want to be learned using our armoury of skills. In a previous book in the series we have looked at learning achieved through insightful questioning and through effective explaining. In this book the emphasis has been on setting tasks which make demands on students' cognitive processes. Whatever method we choose for the lesson – these or others – it has to be handled with skill. This book has suggested that the best tasks have to planned to meet the needs and match the abilities of the learners, and it has offered some insights into the skills of setting tasks.

In turn, the processes of meeting and matching mean that one task is often unlikely to be suitable for every student. The 'one size fits all' of the retail trade is hardly a professional slogan for developing young minds. So differentiation is needed to try to match tasks more effectively to need. It is a subtle business, as teachers have identified in the research which was reported in Chapters 8 and 9.

As we move towards the next millennium there can be little doubt that public and political involvement in schools will increase rather than diminish. This is not a bad thing, though it sometimes is thought to be so. But it does turn the spotlight on any inadequacies in teaching and learning. For the professionals that means that they have to be increasingly sure of their skills, able to articulate why they act as they do, and secure in taking control of their own profession and of their own professional development. It is as a contribution to this process that this teaching skills' series is offered.

Index